DEAR BODY, THANK YOU

Also by Jessica Juliano:

The Worthy Woman Handbook: 28 steps to deeper acceptance, confidence, and trust

Worthy of Me: Reclaiming wholeness from loss to love

Message from the author:

All of my books are available online at bookshop.org. The next time you shop for books, consider supporting a local independent bookstore. They can usually special order any book for you. Prefer to shop online? Visit bookshop.org where every purchase supports an independent bookstore of your choice.

DEAR BODY, THANK YOU

Nurturing a relationship with the body through love letters

JESSICA JULIANO

Jessica Juliano

Book design, cover art, and inside artwork by Jessica Juliano. All photographs are property of the author.

This book is creative nonfiction. The thoughts and ideas in this book are in no way intended to be used in place of expert medical attention and advice. The information and events in this book have been expressed and written as remembered by the author. Names and identifying details have been changed to protect the privacy of individuals.

Juliano, Jessica.
Dear Body, Thank You: Nurturing a relationship with the body through love letters / Jessica Juliano.
ISBN (Paperback) 979-8-8690-1596-9
ISBN (Ebook) 979-8-8690-1597-6
1. Self-Help - Eating Disorders & Body Image. 2. Body, Mind & Spirit - Inspiration & Personal Growth. 3. Self-Help - Journaling.

Published in the USA
First Printing, 2024

For information about permission to reproduce selections from this book or to inquire about special rates for bulk purchases, please contact the author at jessicajulianocoaching@gmail.com.

To my mamasita for showing me that with a little bit of love, we can witness a relationship blossom.

Contents

An Invitation

Dear Body, Thank You was born out of my desire to do two things:

One - Share an honest account about my relationship with my body and how beautifully and painfully complex it can be. From my position as an overthinker and anxiety survivor, combined with external influences like the media and other people's opinions, it's no wonder I've felt crazy as I've struggled to care for my body and figure out what she needs! My hope is to help someone else realize that they are not alone or isolated in their experiences with their body, and that they too can become liberated from external and internal pressures and learn to make choices that better serve them.

Two - Encourage others to connect with their own bodies and inner voices for guidance. My principle has always been that I'm not here to tell anyone else what to do or how to live their life. However, I can offer my personal stories with thoughtful questions to help guide you in finding your own answers. The body is a gift and a miracle. It is worth the investment of time to explore our feelings towards it and the experiences that have shaped our relationship with it. When we open up the lines of communication with our bodies, we may find the answers we seek, and more.

The one suggestion I offer is to read this book with openness. I believe our experiences, no matter how different, can actually highlight our similarities and help us build connections. We may start in different places and travel unique paths, but we all have opportunities to work toward love and acceptance. I only know the world from my body's perspective. It's possible that you may disagree with something I've shared here. Even as the author, I may one day disagree with myself and what I wrote! I'm constantly changing, as are you, and everything around us. I believe if we are willing to lean into the emotions and reactions from hearing someone else's story, we can expand our compassion for all humans, ourselves included.

I invite you to reflect on the stories in this book and consider how your body may be communicating with you. Each section of this book is followed by a letter I wrote to my body as well as a prompt for you to write your own. Most of us have written a letter to another person at some point, but likely not to our own body. The idea is when you write to your body as if it were another person, you can uncover the words that you may be speaking unconsciously to yourself by transferring them onto paper. This can illuminate the nature of the relationship you have with your body. From there, you get to decide what happens next. May the practice of letter writing allow you to connect with your body on a new level and honor that connection as a life-long relationship. As with all relationships, when our actions around our bodies are rooted in respect, patience, and open communication, we can grow acceptance, trust, and love.

May this experience serve you well and help you to uncover the secret recipe for your own harmonious relationship with your body.

All my love,
Jessica

Introduction: Power Couple

What does it mean to have a body? What an enormous responsibility and privilege. To fully appreciate having a body, try imagining life without it.

Only with a body can we experience the grandest and simplest pleasures of life on Earth. We can feel the rush of the wind in our face as we run down a hill. We can taste the flesh of a strawberry bursting in our mouth. Only with a body can we feel the sun's warmth on our skin and hear the melody of ocean waves. A body allows us to snuggle kitties and puppies and experience an interspecies connection. Through the body, the energy of music and movement invigorates and ignites us. We can tremble and soften at the touch of a loved one, inhale their scent, feel their heartbeat. We can experience the racing of our own heart as we step into unknown territory and the surge of confidence as we surmount new challenges and grow stronger.

With a body, we also experience pain and suffering. We may criticize our bodies for not being a certain way and making us feel less than enough. We may get lost in comparison and judgment as we look to others to determine what our bodies should be able to do or how they should look. We may feel frustrated, cheated, and resentful when an illness or injury confines us and keeps us from living our lives. We can become angry with the physical limitations the body imposes as we lose our youthful glow and agility. We are only here for as long as the body permits. We may feel a deep sense of fear about the loss of someone we love or our own eventual death.

To have a body is to be vulnerable to our surroundings.

Everything we consume through our nose, mouth, skin, ears, eyes, and our own minds has a profound impact on our wellbeing. Are we mindful about what we're consuming or have we let the gates down? Are our habits helping us grow stronger or weaker? How can we maintain a peaceful harmony, if there is such a thing?

If you were to write a recipe for a harmonious relationship, what ingredients would you put into the mix? Respect, trust, compassion, and support are at the top of my list. Imagining you're in a relationship with your body creates an opportunity to see how you show up in the relationship. Are you providing your partner, your body, with the support it needs? Do you listen to it with respect and compassion? Do you trust what it tells you?

The relationship with our body is unique in that it's a relationship with ourselves. If you're like me, you may try to control situations or people around you to create a sense of safety. For me, that tendency to control extended to my body. It seemed like it should be easy to get what I wanted and create that safety I craved because my body is a part of me. But it's a part of me that is very wise, and trying to control it for so long cut me off from that great wisdom. I began looking to others to tell me what to do to care for my body, but that left me even more confused and anxious. Have you experienced that, too?

What can we do instead?

We can return to that inner wisdom and choose how we show up at any moment. Like all relationships, those involved may change and grow over time. What the body needs to function at an optimal level may look different at various stages of life or even from day to day. The investment we make in building a foundation of love and respect will carry us through the inevitable changes and challenges, just like a marriage! Some days will be joyful and effortless. Others, we might long for the days we were "single." But there's no breaking up with the body.

The sensations and changes I noticed within my body over recent years called my attention. I am a sensitive person, and I've come to realize that not everyone shares this level of sensitivity. For example, some are able to tune out pain. Not me. When pain became a common communication tool of my body, I realized my only options were to suffer or to listen with love and see how I could better care for myself. For a long time it felt like a burden to feel so much. I thought I was the only one going through such intense experiences in my body. I now know that is not true at all.

I see the body as a blessing and a burden, bringing both pleasure and discomfort. But isn't that the human experience: a spectrum of highs and lows, ebbs and flows, and everything in between? Perhaps then the body is the perfect vehicle to carry us through life. It can be our greatest teacher and ally if we learn to trust and respect it.

When I think about my relationship with my body now, I feel a deep sense of reverence. My body is sacred to me. I know there will be more challenges ahead but now I look forward to meeting them with love and grace. What a gift to have this body. What an honor.

* * *

Dear Body,
Thank you. Thank you for all that you are. I wouldn't change a thing.

I

Smashing Clocks

A typical afternoon in 4th grade went like this. After school, I'd hop off the bus, rush the half-mile trek home through the neighborhood, burst through the front door, head straight for the kitchen, and go digging through the snacks cabinet. We had Dunkaroos, Gushers, fruit snacks, and so many other goodies to choose from. I'd pick two or three and devour them in minutes. The only evidence of my snack attack sat in my lap: empty wrappers and crumbs.

An hour later my mom would call me. "Jeeessicaaaa! Time for dinner!"

I wasn't hungry. I'd just eaten!

As my fork poked and prodded the food on my dinner plate, my mom would ask me, "Why did you eat so much when you knew dinner would be ready soon?"

I was hungry when I got home. How do I tell my body to hold my hunger until 5:30?

At that young age, I didn't recognize that this is common for adults. They adjust their personal schedules to fit around culturally accepted mealtimes. Breakfast at 8, lunch at 12, and dinner at 5:30. Still, I had enough smarts about me to listen to my body and question anyone who told me to do something that was contrary to that. I hadn't yet been brainwashed.

As we grow older we adopt the norms of our culture. It can happen so seamlessly that we don't realize it. One of those norms is to outsource decisions about our routines and wellbeing to clocks, weather apps, abrupt time changes, and scales. It's become normal for numbers to dictate the patterns of our lives.

In my 20s, I almost got fired for being hungry. I worked at a small grocery store while putting myself through massage therapy school. It was late morning and I was standing around the register with my co-workers during a lull. My stomach grumbled. I'd eaten oatmeal for breakfast but it wasn't enough to hold me over until lunch. I looked at the clock. My break wouldn't come for another hour or two. I told my coworker I was going to run to the back room to grab a snack.

While I was taking in a few spoonfuls of yogurt, a manager walked in. "I keep seeing you back here eating. You're supposed to be at the register."

"I'm hungry and needed a snack," I said, guilty that I got caught. "I'm not sure what else to do."

"Okay," he said calmly. "I just don't want this becoming a habit."

I felt myself fighting back tears. What if it *did* become a habit? What if I lost my job? How can I get in trouble for feeling hungry and doing something about it? My metabolism doesn't know what a clock is. Nothing had changed since my 4th grade after-school snack attacks.

Thankfully hunger never cost me my job. Soon after that confrontation with the manager, I graduated from massage school. I started a new job at a spa where I had a small break after every client. Food breaks were not regulated there, so I enjoyed them throughout the day.

Eight years later I returned to my background in IT and worked at a software company. I could take my lunch break whenever I wanted and snack at my desk. No food police there either!

I can't imagine being in healthcare, emergency response, or other professions where people rarely have the flexibility to listen to their bodies for mealtimes or other needs. Nurse friends have told me stories of stashing nuts in their pockets to munch on when they can and barely squeezing in bathroom breaks. They may work an entire 12-hour shift with just a 15 minute break. For some, it's become a luxury to listen to their bodies.

While in recent years I've been able to eat *when* I wanted, I didn't always allow myself to eat *what* I wanted. I spent too many years letting the scale dictate whether or not my body was healthy and if I should be eating more or less. When I stepped on that square platform in the bathroom, the number revealed to me was of utmost importance; more so than energy, satiation, strength, or anything else I could sense on the inside. I've long since come to my senses and haven't owned a scale in years.

My life has revolved around other numbers, too. Not long ago, I developed a weather app addiction. Like a stock day trader, I'd check the weather on my phone throughout the day, hoping to see a number that would please me. It was just like the scale. When I want to know how to dress for an outing, instead of just walking out the front door, I pick up my phone. I don't live in a high rise. My front door opens to the outside. It would take less than a minute to step out. Why do I trust the number on my phone more than the feeling of the air against my skin? If the weather app tells me it's going to be a hot and humid 90 degree day, I'm upset before I've even had the chance to experience it for myself. I might go outside later and find that there's actually a pleasant breeze. Too bad I had already wasted the morning feeling disappointed. I'd given too much power to the weather app. Society has taught me that happiness, or lack thereof, comes from outside of me. The number on the scale. The approval of my boss. The temperature. It's not within my control.

One day, I woke up and had an epiphany. "This is absurd! Why do we do this? Why do we follow these systems that go against what feels good in our bodies?" It was a March morning. Time to spring forward and set the clocks ahead one hour. Many people would be losing an hour of sleep. Many people would be cranky, annoyed, and tired for weeks. I was tired of being one of those people. Of all the ways numbers dictate our lives, this one pissed me off the most.

When I traded in my 8 to 5 office job for a flexible work-from-home gig, I stopped obeying the time changes of spring and fall. How do I tell my body the world is now operating one hour earlier?

I refused to change the clock on my stove and car for weeks. My husband Carlos laughed at me. "Just accept it, mi amor!"

"I will *not* give in to something that doesn't make sense!"

I stood my ground firmly. Well, as best as I could.

Unfortunately, I was not immune to the senseless change accepted by the world around me. While I didn't need a clock with the updated GMT offset to go to bed or wake up in the morning, I did for work meetings and social activities. I tried solving this problem with time travel. I began living in two time zones at once and venturing back and forth between them throughout the day.

Have you ever seen any time travel movies? They leave your head spinning. You think you're following along. There's a clever explanation or alibi for when someone goes back or forward in time and reconnects with their present body later. But as you think about the details afterward, you realize something doesn't quite add up. A lot of unanswered questions remain.

My own time travel experience left me just as confused. I'd say things like "It's 9 AM which means it's *really* 8 AM. Or wait, I mean

10 AM? No, it's really 8 AM. Whatever, the store *should* be open. Let's go." Carlos would just shake his head and grab the keys as we headed to the grocery store to grab some snacks.

Despite my protest against changing the clocks, it was impossible to keep it up when the rest of the country (except the smart folks in Hawaii and Arizona) shifted an hour. Cafes didn't obey what I considered to be the real time. Restaurants didn't open for dinner at my 5 PM because to them it was 4 PM. Our phones and computers switch the time automatically. Our appliances and cars can be adjusted with the press of a few buttons. But there's no switch or button to tell my body to shift my entire schedule by an hour! I still want to go to sleep at 10:30. I still want to wake up at 7:30. And don't you dare make me start working before 9, which to my body is 8! Or is it 10?

After two weeks, I caved and adjusted the clocks.

We look to the clock to tell us when it's the right time to do anything - eat, sleep, exercise, drink coffee, drink wine, have sex, socialize. But the clock is not my body. The clock is not my god. I will wake up, not when some external device rings loudly, but when my body feels rested. I will adjust what or how much I eat, not when a scale reveals a certain number, but when my body tells me she is in need of a change. I will eat, not when I have a break in my busy work schedule, not when my boss says it's acceptable, and not when someone tells me dinner is ready. I will eat when my *body* tells me she's ready. I will operate on my schedule, and I hope you're able to operate on yours, which probably differs from mine. If you're kind enough to invite me over for dinner, I will be kind enough to eat just one little snack to hold me over. I might also bring an appetizer to share in case your body runs on a later dinner schedule and you prefer we chat for a while first. We can learn to respect not just the unique needs of our own bodies, but also those of everyone else.

When we recognize that every human body has unique needs,

we can better understand our own bodies. We can understand how important it is to look within rather than outside of ourselves for guidance. It's a massive hurdle to filter out the noise which comes not only from measurement systems of time, temperature, and weight, but also from the media.

Some people think they know our bodies better than we do and sometimes we believe them. I'm not talking about personalized guidance from a healthcare professional. I'm talking about those in the media trying to convince us that the exact plan they followed to lose weight, improve their health, and rid themselves of [insert any unwanted symptom here] is the plan that will work to get you those same results. A lot of these people mean well and just want to help others feel as good as they do. But since we're all unique, one method won't work for everyone. This is why we have to be cautious about what messages we take in regarding our health and bodies.

Recently I'd heard some health experts advise to allow at least 12 hours of non-eating time overnight. Whatever their reasoning, it sounded convincing to me. Health experts can be very good at convincing. Of course I want to take care of my digestive organs and slow the effects of aging! But I looked at the clock, and it was almost 10 PM. I didn't have a substantial dinner and I was hungry. I knew by the rhythms of my body that I'd want breakfast in the morning around 9. That's one hour shy of their 12-hour rule. I ignored the advice and instead I listened to the rumbles in my tummy and had a snack. Screw the damn clock!

What if I just stopped looking at the clock? I did it with the scale and that was successful. What would it be like to remove all external cues and only listen to those from my body? Aren't my body's cues designed to guide me? What if I could open my brain and dump out all of the useless knowledge that's been force fed to me about how I should care for my body? If I could do this even for a day, oh what I could learn!

Goals, rules, habits, clocks, and numbers do serve a purpose, though. They can provide us with a healthy level of encouragement, accountability, and structure. If I see I've walked 2200 steps, I may push myself a little more to 2500 or 3000. If I see it's almost 9:30 PM, I'll close my laptop and get ready for bed so I get enough sleep. For someone with a legitimate reason to adjust their weight, the scale can be a motivating way to track progress. But we may at times cross that sneaky line where using a number to encourage us shifts into judging ourselves. That's what we can be mindful of. We may think we haven't done enough unless we attain a certain level or number. We may feel our efforts don't count if we don't meet a minimum time requirement. We may feel really cranky for days as we try to adjust to a time change forced upon us.

When we turn to an external device or system to dictate what our bodies should be able to handle, we are outsourcing our truth. Let's take this opportunity to remember and honor the natural and changing rhythms of our bodies. Perhaps listening before acting can teach us more about our bodies than any number or device can.

* * *

Dear Body,

You are my source of truth. You are a miracle. You tell me what you need. You are a powerful communicator. It's just that I've been taught to stop listening. I've been taught to believe what other people's bodies want is what you want. It's gotten so muddled. I used to try to force you to wait to eat because I thought that was right. But you just wanted to be fed. I used to think I should be able to do intense things in the morning before it got too hot, but you always felt weak and I got mad at you for that. Now as I stopped forcing, and made choices out of love, I can see how strong you are. You are my guide. You are my source of truth. I vow to respect you. You hold all the answers. Thank you, dear Body. Thank you.

Letter Prompt

How do numbers like the clock, scale, or others affect your routine? How does your body respond to that? If your body ran your schedule, what would your day look like? Use the space below to write a letter to your body.

2

I've Got a Hot Bod

It cost me a \$95 visit to my acupuncturist to understand that if something is uncomfortable to the point that I think I might pass out, die, or experience harm in any way, I should probably stop doing it.

Once we grow out of our fearless youth, this should become common sense, right? Perhaps I missed something.

For someone like me who loves the outdoors and grows anxious when trapped inside all day, Florida summers have become something to fear. This is especially so during a pandemic where there are few indoor air-conditioned spaces to escape to. Working and living full-time from home, I had nowhere to go until after sunset.

In March 2021, summer descended upon us early with temperatures in the mid-80s. I had a melt down. I'd been seeing a practitioner of acupuncture and Chinese medicine for a few months for anxiety, a battle I'd been fighting since my dad passed in 2017. During my last visit, I told him about my fear of the summer heat. I left with this wisdom: If it's hot outside and I think it might not be a good idea to exercise outdoors, then I should keep myself safely inside with the comfort of my AC. I may see others doing what I think I should be able to do, but what they can do has nothing to do with me. Not even if I see someone twice my age hauling ass on their 65-mile daily bike ride, barely breaking a sweat in their helmet and long-sleeved shirt. Not even if I see someone who looks overweight, pushing themselves to run in their sweat-soaked t-shirt. It has nothing to do with me. Not even if I see someone who looks like me taking a long walk just as I had planned to do, it doesn't matter. I don't like the heat, so I should go inside.

Regardless of what anyone else is doing or appears to be doing, if my body feels hot and uncomfortable, and I think the heat is too much, I should go inside. That would be better and wiser than pushing myself to the end of my workout, all the while fueling the anxious thoughts of "What if I'm overexerting myself? What if I pass out? What if someone finds me on the sidewalk and has to call an ambulance?" Going inside would be better. It's just plain common sense.

Then, why did I push myself?

There's a very influential theme in our culture of pushing through obstacles. We have catchy phrases like "No pain no gain!", "Master your mindset!", and "No excuses!" It's easy to think that we can and should test our limits. But does that overtake common sense or our own ability to decide what's best for us in a given moment?

There's a time and place for everything. It's one thing to push myself in a workout when I know it's safe to do so. If I'm just not feeling motivated one day, it's easy to succumb to excuses like "I'm tired" or "I'm bored" and make plans to quit early to go home and relax on the couch. In those moments, I can harness the power of my thoughts by telling myself how strong and capable I am so I keep going and build my endurance. Catchphrases like "Master your mindset!" or "Don't be a quitter!" can be useful gamechangers. It's another matter to push through my body feeling very hot, ignoring her cues, and making myself feel worse. I should have been able to figure that one out on my own. I should have been smarter than that. I *am* smart. I just fell into the same trap as many of us do.

Those catchphrases and messages from society about pushing through spoke louder in my mind than my own thoughts and body signals. I looked at those around me and made judgments about myself based on what I saw. I decided I should be able to do what they're doing. I thought I was just using the heat as an excuse, and I shouldn't let that stop me. I didn't want to be a quitter.

Comparison can motivate us. It can also be dangerous and cause us to stop making decisions for ourselves. We may take what other people feed us without asking if that is what we or our bodies want. We can become so desperate for guidance yet can't connect with our own sources of guidance like body cues, intuition, or common sense. We just want someone else to tell us what to do. Why do we trust *them* more?

Three years of anxiety left me so disconnected from my body that I stopped trusting her. Anxiety feels like my body is working against me. It feels like the whole world is a death trap that I could fall into at any moment. Why would I listen to that? Instead, I listened to anyone who seemed smart and mentally sound. If they weren't crippled by anxiety like me, they must know better.

Sadhguru, a spiritual leader I listened to on occasion, had talked about the importance of committing to our usual tasks and priorities even when feeling unwell. Otherwise, he cautioned, the body would learn to make excuses to rest. Over time it would weaken us. He said to just get up and do what you would do, and the body will adapt that way. It will learn to become stronger.

For a time his words resonated with me. I was tired of feeling weak from anxiety. There were days it was so bad I couldn't go to the grocery store or walk around the block without thinking I might stop breathing and end up in the hospital. Simple tasks challenged me. I wanted a normal life. I wanted to enjoy walking, regardless of the humidity, the UV index, or whether or not I had a headache.

Sometimes trusting Sadhguru's words worked for me. One day I felt quite anxious but trusted I could leave the house, go on a dolphin site-seeing boat cruise, and very likely not die. I was right! The bumpy ride on choppy water almost sent me down a rabbit hole of "I'm not gonna survive this!" But the salty air blowing in my face snapped me out of it. It told me, "Get out of your head! Come back to real life!" After that, I received an unexpected and mesmerizing sight: a pod of dolphins leaping out of the water in unison! What a reward for pushing myself out of my comfort zone that day.

Fast-forward seven months and the anxiety had gotten a lot better. I didn't need to tell myself as often that I could go to the store and pick up some cat food or go for a leisurely bike ride and not die. I was rebuilding the trust between myself and my body. The world was no longer out to get me.

That March morning in 2021, I felt energized and eager to go for a long power walk. When the summer heat smacked me in the face, it awakened that panicky voice that I thought had long departed. The voice told me that it was so hot, I could overexert myself. I might pass out and a passerby would have to call 9-1-1. Sure it was exaggerating, but the underlying message was to protect me. I tried to fight it, reminding myself that it's only March and this is ridiculous! But my body felt hot.

I remembered what Sadhguru had said: to not give in, to not let the body get weak. I watched 70-year-olds pass me, running with their sweat bands and tanned legs. "You can do this!" I thought to myself. "If you think this is too hot, how are you going to survive the next seven months? You've got to build your body up and get used to this!"

I convinced myself to stay out for 30 minutes, all the while not sure which voice was right, and feeling terribly anxious and unsure. I went back home and spent the rest of the day inside. Agitated and on the verge of panic, I debated whether or not to turn on the AC. It was 78 degrees inside. Not sweltering, but uncomfortable in both my mind and body. It was only March. I should be able to tolerate this.

That day, Sadhguru's teaching did not resonate with me. I tried to listen to him and pushed myself too far. By listening to him, I ignored my inner knowing and body signals. And for what? Because I wanted to prove my strength? To whom?

There had been many times when I felt unwell and decided to go against his teaching. I've been tired, with a headache, or nursing physical pain. I chose to listen to my body instead and trust her signals that she needed rest. I knew that pushing through to exercise or work late would not serve me well. But alas I'm human, and some days I forget.

When I recounted this steamy tale to my acupuncturist, and he told me to avoid the heat and go inside, it seemed silly that I ever considered otherwise. Now I laugh at the $95 visit - money that I could have applied to my electric bill instead - but it was a lesson I needed. It even tamed the thermostat battle between me and my husband. He likes it cold. I like to conserve energy. I got personal and relationship counseling in one session!

A few days later I was out biking with my friend Nate through the beach town of Gulfport. We pedaled past colorful cottages on an old brick road. The atmosphere felt ripe for one of our soul-nourishing discussions. With excitement, I recounted this story to him about my revelation of listening to my body. Secretly I was also testing out material for this book. I awaited his affirming reaction.

In response, Nate seemed to agree with Sadhguru. He said, "The only way out is through. You just gotta do it." Meaning, I had to finish my walk in the heat to overcome my fear of it.

But was I afraid of the heat? Maybe not. Maybe it was just my body saying "Hey, this doesn't feel good. Let's do something else."

Maybe we don't always have to push through or persevere or make ourselves stronger. Instead, why don't we listen to our bodies and then decide? What if, by communicating with our bodies, we could tell the difference between a cue to stop what we're doing and an excuse of laziness? The challenge is listening, really listening, and knowing and trusting ourselves enough to choose the right course of action.

When I got home from acupuncture, it was a stuffy 78 degrees inside. I walked to the thermostat and turned on the AC. I could have tolerated the day without it, but I've got a hot bod.

* * *

Dear Body,

What is so uncomfortable about being uncomfortable? How can one day sweating in the sun and building strength feel so good and empowering and healing, and another day I fear it will be the death of me? How can this be? Well, for one, heat stroke! I'm not crazy for being scared. My body is protecting me against a real threat of the Florida climate. I know you are so much stronger and capable than I realize, but that doesn't mean I can put myself at risk and breeze through it just by telling myself I can do it. Maybe that works for some people, but I'm not them. I thank you, my body and mind, for protecting me. I am learning to distinguish when my mind is keeping me safe from a real threat and I should listen to it, and when it is simply scared to experience something new and it is safe to lean into the discomfort. Thank you for being my teacher.

Love,
Me

Letter Prompt

Is there a situation presenting a conflict between what your body feels and what others do or say? Use this space to write a letter to your body to explore this conflict.

3

How Do You Measure Perfection?

"Look at that forehead!" My grandma pushed my hair out of my eyes and ran her fingers around the perimeter of my face. "You girls are so lucky!" she exclaimed, admiring my sister and I for what seemed like a rather uninteresting part of the body.

"My forehead is huge. Look at this!" My aunt swept her bangs up and exposed herself. "I've always had to wear bangs to hide it. You girls have such nice small foreheads. You don't even need bangs."

Before then, I had no idea there was an ideal forehead size. Thankfully I'd been blessed with a good one and didn't have to give it another thought until now. Nearly 25 years later, I'm reflecting upon why I've expected my body to be perfect in so many ways. During those 25 years, I discovered plenty of other parts and characteristics to worry about that did not meet the ideal criteria. This led me down a path of suffering, obsessive controlling habits, and on some days, deep reverence and acceptance.

If you were to get your hands on my 5th grade class photo, I'd be the one in the middle row on the right side with greasy hair, matching baby barrettes, glasses, and braces. Only one of those was in style at the time. Perhaps that's why I chose to hide myself inside a Tommy Hilfiger t-shirt two sizes too large for my tiny frame. Tomboy fashion was in, lucky for me. Those clashing pink bow barrettes were my only claim to femininity; a tiny breadcrumb in case I disguised myself beyond recognition. It was easier to go the route of baggy boyish clothes when I felt I had no chance of measuring up to the tall, pretty, athletic cheerleaders that stole the attention of my male classmates. They didn't get the memo that I had the best forehead this side of the Mississippi. If I chose to hide, it would hurt less when others didn't see me.

That same year I noticed that I was a bit pudgy compared to the other girls. This put an idea in my head that I could stand to lose some weight. No one called me fat or teased me about my weight. I received the message loud and clear that thin was in from the super skinny fashion models strutting around on TV and magazine covers.

My mom must have received the same message. She stashed SlimFast shakes in the pantry and constantly talked about needing to lose a few pounds. One time, my sister and I snuck a shake when Mom was at work. We sat on the couch and passed it between us like a joint. It tasted like cardboard and chocolate milk, but we drank it. Unlike my first actual joint, I had no desire to drink another SlimFast shake. We were much happier years later when Mom switched to SnackWell's Devil's Food cookies.

If you asked me, I would've said that my desire to lose weight began with a positive intention to be healthier. I made small adjustments like eating sandwiches without mayonnaise and refraining from margarine, which seemed like good choices. But the encouragement didn't come from messages about how eating healthier foods would help me. It came from messages about how I should look a certain way.

After school, I'd spend time on the treadmill, Nordic Rider, stationary bike, or whatever exercise machine trend my dad had bought into that he hadn't yet converted into a coat rack. While watching TV and movies, I'd pedal with gusto. I felt proud that I was doing something good for myself. I once watched the entire *Save the Last Dance* movie while running on the treadmill. The endorphins of my workout combined with the feel-good ending of the movie convinced me that I was a champion. But my workout was fueled in part by something else. I stared at the lead actress, Julia Stiles, who frequently bared her tiny midriff in the movie. In the back of my mind, I thought the faster I ran, the closer I'd get to being her.

As time went on, my initial positive intention got lost. I had indeed lost weight, and it was going so well that it gave me a power trip. I took more drastic measures to keep it going. My actions revealed that I'd gone toward the dark side. While the other kids were happily eating their lunches in the school cafeteria, I chose not to eat. Like a drug dealer, I started a side hustle selling my lunch snacks for 25 cents. Those kids went crazy for their Dunkaroos! Other items didn't sell so well, such as my turkey sandwiches. I stashed them, untouched, in the bottom drawer of my bedroom dresser. I felt too guilty to throw them in the trash, knowing my mom spent the time making them for me. At the time I was impressed with the results I was getting. In retrospect, the only impressive thing about this is that my room never developed a mold or ant problem.

Over time, I grew out of skipping meals. The thought of my parents finding out filled me with guilt and shame. It was enough to make me quit cold turkey. With that, I began eating cold turkey sandwiches again.

In my 20s, the power trip I felt in controlling and shaping my body continued in another way. I cared less about my weight and being skinny. Strong became the new sexy! I wanted to look like the fitness icons with their perfect abs and low body fat percentage. My dream body was now slightly muscular and toned. That meant I had to lift weights and log lots of time on the elliptical machine. I had to work even harder to compensate for all the alcohol I consumed on the weekends.

When I got really disciplined about my body goals, I ditched the alcohol, the friends that went with it, and many joys in my life. Most people my age enjoyed going out to dinner with friends. You know, that casual pastime of laughing, talking and relaxing over a nice meal and a beverage or two. Casual is the opposite of disciplined. Restaurants presented a huge risk. I couldn't control what I ate at a restaurant. Anything on the menu would surely go against my strict dietary guidelines. I had no room for "casual" in my plan. Restaurants went immediately to the "NO" list, right under pizza. Except on Sundays. Pizza could only be consumed on Sundays.

People told me they admired my willpower when it came to diet and exercise. They hadn't a clue the trade off I was making. On the outside it looked like I was tenacious, dedicated, and determined. But none of those words described me. I was driven by an obsessive need to control. To be what I thought I needed to be to be good enough. To be liked. To be seen.

My girlfriend at the time saw me all right. She observed my controlling behavior and told me I was no fun to be around. Now I can appreciate her frankness in calling me out on it. But back then I was too narrow minded to listen to reason. She tried to throw me a lifeline, inviting me back to the civilized crowd who ate tacos not just on Tuesdays but sometimes on Wednesdays as well. I refused.

Despite my efforts, I could only maintain this strict regimen for a few weeks at a time, a month tops if I was really motivated. Something would always happen to derail me. I'd get a cold or feel exhausted and grant myself permission to take a day's rest from my exercise plan. The break would be so welcome that I wouldn't want to go back. Ever! As strict as I was, I allowed that to happen. My breaks from exercise could last for months! But eventually something would remind me of how shameful I felt my habits were, how lazy I'd become, and how far I'd strayed from the pursuit of the beautiful sexy body I wanted. I wasn't enough as I was. I had to do and be better. The pressure would convince me to get back on the wagon.

Wash, rinse, repeat.

One day while hanging out with my friend Dani, she told me about her new job. She was actually balancing two jobs to pay her student loans and some financial debt her ex-husband had left her. "I love all the experience I'm getting, but I'm not sure how long I can keep it up." She explained. "It's not sustainable."

Sustainable. My mind took a highlighter and colored all over this word as if I had been searching for it for so long. But why? Up until that point I'd only heard or used that word in reference to caring for our planet. Dani used it in the context of how our everyday habits affect our wellbeing and whether or not we can maintain that over a long period of time. "Sustainable" echoed in my head like a mantra for days. My brain organized a special focus group to decode its relevance to the conscious part of me. Finally, the right brain cells fired, the connection was made, and the focus group delivered on its mission. I recognized that my habits with eating and exercise were absolutely *not* sustainable. I thought I was being healthy and yet, my back and forth, on again off again approach, was incredibly *unhealthy*. Health should be something we do every day. It should be a habit. A lifestyle. It should be *sustainable*. It's not pulling an all-nighter to cram for an exam because you spent the last month goofing off. Health is a practice, a lifelong commitment. Our bodies deserve to be treasured for the lifetime we have with them. I was not treasuring my body. I was punishing her.

Upon this realization, I relaxed quite a bit. I decided that it was okay to eat carbs. I allowed myself to eat fruit every day, along with a big bowl of oatmeal or rice. Yep, I was living on the wild side. There might even be photographic evidence somewhere of me eating pizza on a Tuesday! With cheesy crust!

While my outer habits may have changed, it wasn't enough to shield me from society's pressure to be a certain way. By my 30s, I'd made peace with how my body looked. I loved her, appreciated her, and took good care of her. My primary motivation with exercise was no longer to shape the physical appearance of my body because I no longer succumbed to the lure of fitness models and celebrities. I exercised because I loved to move and it felt good. It made me feel free, strong, energized, and alive. But I also did it because I knew it was good for me. The pressure I felt to have a perfect body turned to the inside. With the reach of the Internet, suddenly I found myself on email lists and social media accounts sharing the latest health advice. I became obsessed with being healthy, as healthy as I could possibly be. I wanted all my organs and internal systems to operate at their optimal state. I made changes to my diet in an attempt to achieve perfect health.

On occasion, I'd use online calculators and tools to track my daily food consumption to make sure I was getting proper amounts of vitamins and minerals. When I discovered that my vitamin C intake was low (due to an online tool, not a blood test or personalized assessment from a doctor), I freaked! Isn't that supposed to be one of the easiest nutrients to get? I eat fruit! At least I was mindful enough to stop myself from searching the web for the symptoms of low vitamin C. Instead, I ate more bell peppers.

There's so much information everywhere we look, bombarding us every second of the day. There are lists of foods and habits that are "so bad" for us, we need to eliminate them immediately if we want any chance of living long enough to see our grandchildren. Then there are the lists of what will make us "so healthy and vibrant," we should drop everything we're doing right this second and start doing them now. We are constantly told what diseases we are at risk of contracting and how damaging the toxins and pesticides are in our food. Is anything safe?

I became obsessed with cutting out processed foods and sugar to the point that I could hardly enjoy anything I ate. This period of my life saddened me because I've always loved food. I loved trying different flavors, savoring each bite, and the simple experience of eating. I lost that joy. Sure, the foods I prepared tasted good. It's not like I was eating steamed spinach and chicken breast with no salt or seasoning (thankfully those days were long gone). I made delicious adventurous food! Chicken and cabbage salad in a tangy turmeric tahini sauce. Slow-cooked curries with aromatic spices and coconut milk. And truthfully the best hummus I've ever had. (Google "best hummus ever" to find the recipe. It's not a lie!) The meals were nutrient packed, well-balanced, and delicious, but my thoughts collided with my ability to fully enjoy them. "What if I'm consuming too much cholesterol? Is it bad to eat chicken twice a day? What if I'm eating too many nuts and nut butters? What if that clogs my arteries? Is it bad to have yogurt after a bowl of sautéed greens? I just read that calcium inhibits nutrient absorption and I want to absorb my greens!"

Eventually I came to my senses and took proper action. I stopped using ambiguous online tools. I cut back on searching the Internet for health advice. I scrolled past ads and videos about the latest food trends.

For the first time in my adult life, I agreed to the annual blood work recommended by my doctor. I had put it off for a while because I didn't like the idea of my delicate arm being pricked, but for the sake of sanity and reliable data, I gave in. The results revealed there was nothing wrong with my vitamin C. In fact most of the items were in the expected range. Despite the good news, this only relaxed me for a few weeks. There was always something else to convince me I had to do better and keep my cycle of control going.

My obsessive worrying peaked in response to the 2020 COVID-19 pandemic. It seemed more crucial than ever to eat an extremely healthy diet to keep my immune system strong. It was no longer enough to know my blood work was in good shape. I wanted all my organs and internal systems to be functioning optimally. But how does one even measure this?

I'd ponder how great it'd be to have a device to track the quality of my health, something beyond smartwatches that only track heart rate and how many calories you burn. I wanted to know how to maintain an A+ on daily operations. I pressured my body to be perfectly healthy and yet perfectly healthy is not even something that we can define or measure. The closest I could get might require spending hours hooked up to machines, confined to a hospital bed and small room with sad paintings on the walls.

I wanted to know the measures I could take to keep my body in tip-top health. Yet, the more access I got to this kind of information, the more I panicked. The more anxiety I felt. The harder it became to make sound choices about what I ate. Nothing seemed safe anymore. All because I wanted my body to be a perfect, disease-fighting, nutrient-absorbing, energy-building machine. "Why?" I asked myself in earnest. Why had that become so important to me? How did I get to be this way? What was I hoping to achieve... Or escape? Why wasn't a perfect forehead enough?

With the right question, the right answer comes.

The response I felt inside was that I did all of this so that I'd never have to feel badly. I would never have to feel *uncomfortable*. Just like the girl in 5th grade who hid behind oversized t-shirts to avoid the pain of not being seen or loved by her peers. I did it to protect myself.

But I was no longer in 5th grade and no longer trying to win the affection of those around me. I discovered there was a new discomfort I didn't want to feel. Death? Was I afraid of dying? No, I realized. Not dying. *Suffering*. I didn't want to suffer. It wasn't about having a perfect body or perfect health. I was trying to shield myself from all the horrible things that could happen to me. There was too much information filling my insides with fear of what could go wrong, of what could cause suffering. It made me crazy. It sucked away my joy.

Ironically, I had this gut feeling that I was in great health and would probably never face any of the health challenges I was trying to avoid. Yet, I knew that if I kept this up, I'd sentence myself to a lifetime of worrying about it. That just might be worse. My acupuncturist summed it up when he told me, "The stress will kill you before the cholesterol does." *Oh shit*. Now, I have to worry about *stress?!*

One year later, I repeated my annual blood work. The night before my doctor's appointment to review the results, I awoke in a panic. Thinking of what he might reveal terrified me, even though I had no reason to expect anything bad. I admitted to him the next day that I felt like a straight A student who just wanted to get an A+ on her blood test. After a thorough review, he looked at me and said, "Yep, you get an A+! I wish my cholesterol was this good!"

I finally got what I wanted. The perfect grade. It took the pressure off, and I relaxed around food again. It was just like the "sustainable" revelation, though. It made me feel better for a little while. Nothing more.

Like an onion, I began to see how there were so many layers to my relationship with my body. I had conquered some, like outer body image, but there would always be another layer. Fear had taken over so much of my life and ran many layers deep. I couldn't rely on a once-a-year blood test to calm me down and reassure me that I was still healthy. I had to look at what lay underneath the need for a perfect grade. "This must be the biggest damn onion on the planet," I thought.

If my fear is suffering, then I must learn to accept that no one can escape suffering in life. It will come to us all. Yes, I can take measures to minimize it. My attempt to control my health stems from the positive intention to feel good for as long as I can. But how much suffering had I caused myself in the process?

Perfection does not exist. It cannot be measured or tracked because it is not real. And even if it was, the agony we put ourselves through in the attempt to attain it probably outweighs any false sense of joy or accomplishment we think we will get. If my life ends tomorrow, I would be grateful that I took good care of my body but would feel sad that I wasted so much time worrying.

The question now is how does one transition away from perfectionist tendencies? The answer comes when I notice how I got there in the first place. I rejected my body as she was. I stopped listening to her and started controlling her. We didn't talk about what I was doing or why. Her opinions and needs didn't matter. I now can see clearly that the first step in healing is to open the lines of communication, to have a dialogue with my body and reset expectations. It was time to rewrite the contract of our relationship.

Let's consider what it means to have a body. It's being in a relationship. What are the responsibilities of this relationship? What do I expect of my body? Perfection is no longer it. And what does my body need from me? A paranoid tyrant is clearly not the answer. But I don't want to drop everything and end up on the opposite end of the spectrum. A lot of the choices I make and have made are good for this relationship. It's the guilt, stress, and fear that get in the way.

So, dear body, let's make a pact between us. Let's commit to listening, acceptance, love, and respect. Let's rebuild our foundation on these values. Let's write a new contract that reflects each of our voices and needs, from forehead to toes and everything in between. Let's do this together.

* * *

Dear Body,

Here's what I expect of you:

- To be the vehicle through which I experience and explore this world for the duration of my human life.
- To communicate to me how you're feeling and when something's in need of attention.
- To use your innate abilities to take care of yourself as best as you can.

Here's what you can expect of me:

- To listen to your forms of communication, knowing this is wisdom from within, and take action to fulfill your needs.
- To trust in you, appreciate and celebrate you, and respect and treasure you as a dear friend.
- To be grateful to you for giving me the gift of experiencing life and all it has to offer.
- To make choices every day that support your well-being. This will at times include challenging you so you can grow stronger.
- To accept that the body changes over time and I'll have to reassess and adapt my care practices.
- To practice self-kindness and compassion, knowing I will do all of this imperfectly.

* * *

Over time I've found that the more I trust my body, the better I feel and the easier it becomes to accept any perceived imperfections. I choose to focus on my body's capability, strength, and resilience as often as I can, though this is challenged often by illness, injury, and the tendency to compare myself to others. We're doing the best we can. Like a marriage, we're building a partnership; not one that's perfect, but one that's sustainable for us both.

Letter Prompt

Explore any expectations you've held of your body, past and present. What's been helpful? What's in need of revision? When you feel ready, write a contract between you and your body.

I
AM
A
WARRIOR

4

Unnerved

My mid-30s is when I became aware of the switch. I'd never seen it. I didn't know where it lived or who controlled it, but I was convinced it existed. Do you know it? The magical switch that dictates when you feel pain and when you feel peace. There's no other explanation for pain that appears and disappears at random. It must be a switch.

I'd been experiencing shooting pain down my right leg. It wasn't a new occurrence for me nor a regular one, but familiar enough that I knew what to expect. That magical switch was in the ON position and I didn't know how to turn it off. I'd have to pop a pain reliever every night before bed for a week if I wanted to sleep. It was my only defense. Otherwise, the pain would keep me awake all night. I'd toss and turn, desperate to find a position where the switch would shut off so I could relax and fall asleep. Such a position did not exist. After five to seven nights of this routine, the pain would mysteriously stop. I didn't know who or what controlled the switch, but something took mercy on me and flipped it.

This time around, for many reasons, I did not want to pop a pill. For one, I found it a bit concerning how resistant I'd grown to feeling pain or discomfort. Having a body means feeling every sort of thing, not all of them pleasant. The unpleasant ones don't mean I'm going to die or live with pain forever, so I'd rather help my body resolve it than pop a pill to block the sensation and forget about it. It's like punishing a child for doing something wrong without talking with her to understand what led her to do it. Blocking pain without understanding its root cause is a punishment to me because I won't learn how to manage or prevent it.

If you've ever experienced nerve pain, you may have also craved what I did: someone to ram their fist so deeply into my leg, they could hit the painful spot dead on and make it go away, like defusing a ticking time bomb. Just make the ticking stop, please, I beg you! I did try such tactics, enlisting a foam roller and my partner's giant hands. My leg muscles loved the attention, but it didn't alleviate the pain. I suspected a bone in my hip was compressing a nerve, but I didn't know where.

While Carlos brewed a strong bitter chamomile tea to help me sleep, I took to the yoga mat. I stretched my low back, hip flexors, quads, IT bands, hamstrings, and many other parts I wasn't acquainted with by name yet. I repeated these stretches three times a day over the next several days.

The pain slowly eased up. Only one night did it cause me to toss and turn. A couple of other nights I slept poorly out of fear that I'd move into a position that would flip the pain switch back on. Luckily that didn't happen.

I felt proud of my choices. I made it through without any pain reliever! Of greater importance, I was learning to listen to my body and establish habits to care for her for a lifetime. I didn't give in to the allure of instant gratification and numbing. "I can do this!"

I realized, "I can talk to the pain and understand what my body needs. Yes!"

Between my thoughts of gratitude, I detected a tinge of dread. *Would I have to do these stretches multiple times a day for the rest of my life?*

I knew the nerve pain would heal, and we'd enjoy a long pleasant vacation away from each other. I also knew my legs tend to stiffen from my work which requires a lot of sitting. So pain or no pain, the answer is yes. I probably would have to do this for the rest of my life. Forever.

When did it become such an inconvenience to take care of my body?

Having legs that function is a blessing. They carry me around through all of my adventures. I can't imagine not having them. Sometimes when I'm walking, I can feel the stiffness in my knee, and I'll think, "Oh my gosh, what if it just breaks?" As if my body were a machine that might crumble and fall apart.

Is it so much to ask to take 20 minutes a day to stretch and cater to the longevity of my miraculous legs?

I recall the first time I had to make such a compromise. I had recovered from a cold and felt great except for a lingering cough. It drove me insane, forcing me to pop cough drops throughout the day just to get a moment's relief. Cherry. Eucalyptus. Honey lemon. I kept the bags on my work desk, rotating the flavors like a candy dispenser.

This was the second time in two years that a cough had lingered for so long. I went to my doctor, seeking an explanation. It turned out stomach acid was the reason for my cough. They called it silent reflux, which is like heartburn but without the burn. I'd never had regular heartburn before and wasn't sure what kind of acid *wouldn't* burn. But that was the kind I had.

I made an appointment with a gastroenterologist. When the

doctor entered the room and saw me sitting on the table, he shook his head sadly and said, "No no no, you are too young to be here!" He handed me a list of foods to remove from my diet. His assistant sent me home with samples of a medication that could control the acid. When I got home, I stuck them in the back of a drawer.

After two months of coughing, it just stopped one day. Did someone turn off the switch? Or had I become too occupied with other things to think of it? At some point I stopped noticing, and before I knew it, it just wasn't there.

When talking about my experience with a nurse practitioner friend, she said stress can be a cause of silent reflux. I thought back to what was going on in my life the two times this happened. The first was after a tumultuous breakup. The second was after my dad's cancer diagnosis. Yep, those were pretty stressful times.

The third occurrence came as no surprise. I caught a cold shortly after my dad passed away, and yet again the cough lingered. I still had those sample pills from the GI doctor in my drawer, but I knew I didn't need them. What I needed was to reduce stress and calm my body. The best way I knew how to do that was to breathe mindfully. Every morning, every night, and any time during the day when I felt I needed to, I sat in quiet and practiced breathing.

My favorite technique is alternate nostril breathing. It requires so much focus that my mind can't think of anything else. It's a mental recess, a meditation. The slow breathing creates a lovely sense of peace and calm in my body. I turned to this practice during grief when I felt too weak to do anything else. Now it's helping those flaps in my esophagus return to their proper position so I could stop coughing.

After two weeks, the coughing stopped; two weeks compared to two months and who knows how many bags of cough drops. I was pretty damn impressed with myself. Through breathing, I had figured out how to heal myself. I had discovered the switch!

Initially, this experience got to my ego. I felt almighty, with a power surging through me that could heal anything. I could control my body! I could make it do what I wanted! This was a dangerous way to see it. Control implies force and doing something that might be harmful. I spent too many years exercising control, trying to get my body to look a certain way, with washboard abs and fitness model contours. I had gotten stuck in a cycle of food deprivation, calorie counting, and over exercising, followed by a crash and burn of eating whatever I wanted, not exercising for months, and sitting on the couch watching mediocre sitcoms. That was how control played out for me. That was definitely not good for my body.

Thankfully, what I'd discovered through this breathing practice was not control at all. There was no forcing of anything. I was learning to listen to my body and ask her what she needed. She was teaching me how to trust. She was showing me that if I placed my trust in her, then together we could find a way to feel our best. We could live and breathe in partnership, as allies. After all, we do everything together. She is what keeps me here. We might as well make decisions together.

As beautiful as that all sounds, I still have days when it feels like such a burden to have to make this commitment over and over. Yes, dear body, today I'll do my stretching. Yes, my love, today I promise to take a break and breathe when I feel stressed. It's annoying to have to constantly step away from the task at hand to move, stretch, breathe, or do whatever it is my body may need at the moment to keep the switch OFF. I could see myself as a slave to my body, living in fear of a nagging cough or a painful nerve ruining my sleep for a week or more.

Or I could see it another way.

What if when we breathe, stretch, massage, eat, exercise, or do any of the things that are meant to care for our bodies, we *don't* think of controlling or being controlled? What if we *don't* think of trying to force the pain to go away or extra calories to burn off? What if instead we think of love? What if we imagined our actions transferring love to all the parts of our beautiful bodies that need it most at that moment? What if we think of replenishing the reserves so that our bodies can feel loved and cared for throughout our lives?

Every morning I go for a walk. I started waking up earlier so I could enjoy this time before the summer heat sends me indoors. Before my walk, I sit on the ground and rub my legs briskly. I used to do this before a run to prevent cramps in my calves. Now I do it to get the blood flowing and to keep my joints happy. This morning as I sat there rubbing my calves and thighs, I thought what a beautiful caring act this is. I imagined my hands glowing with love, respect, and admiration for my legs. That's exactly what I massaged into them.

No, it's not realistic to imagine this all the time. Some days it's too flowery for me. But what if I just remember this *sometimes*?

As I get older, I'm going to need these acts of care more and more. If I'm able to shift my perspective now from burden to love, it can only help me. If I can be an example of taking breaks to calm my body and reduce stress, I can give others permission to do the same. Together we can all feel a little more comfortable and a little more cared for in our bodies.

There's still some mystery around the switch and how it works, but I know it's not a simple ON/OFF switch. There's no secret button or someone I can bribe. It's different each time because my body is different each time. The switch doesn't respond to force or control. It responds to the acts of listening and loving between me and my body. The more I do this, the more the switch fades into the background, and what's left is a woman who will accept whatever her body presents and care for it as best she can.

* * *

Dear Body,

When I don't have the perfect answer or solution, I feel stressed. I feel pressure and tension like I HAVE to come up with something quickly... or else... I'm letting someone down. Maybe I just need to let someone down. I just have to be honest about not having a good answer. At work, why do I think I'm getting paid to be perfect? People are relying on me and paying me. I equate receiving money with "I have to deliver perfectly or else they'll want their money back, and I need money too." It takes courage to STOP working and being productive and earning money to sit here with myself, with my body. It takes compassion to say "This is important - I love you and you deserve to heal." And of course I am connecting with myself in the process. This is how I heal. This is what makes me feel better. Stopping, witnessing, listening. This is my gift.

I
Accept
+
Allow
what
is

Letter Prompt

What acts of care make a helpful difference in how you feel? How can you and your body continue building your partnership together? If you're ever unsure, consider asking your body, verbally or through writing, and allow it to respond to you.

Morning Prayer

I rise
just after the sun
My little pink bike
and my blessed legs
give me a tour of nature's treasures
I see the slugs retiring from their morning stroll
Hear the birds exchanging pleasantries over breakfast
Jasmine and plumeria speak in scents
offering their fine fragrance
as good day wishes
I reach my destination: the top of the bridge
The still waters of the bay
beckon me to rest
before the day carries me away
On the journey home
the wind cools my skin's tears of joy
I rise
and I give thanks
to my body
and the world that bore her

5

Burning Bridges

As a teenager, my wildest daydreams centered around Usher. The smooth and sexy R&B singer made me wanna do all kinds of things nice and slow. I imagined that one day during lunch, the principal would enter the cafeteria and surprise us with a concert by a special guest. The lights would dim and the spotlight would shine down on a microphone stand. Usher would strut out in tight leather pants, grin dreamily at all of us, and grab that microphone in his hand like he was ready to make love to it. He'd cast his gaze over the crowd until his eyes settled on the one person he found irresistible. Me. He'd beckon me to join him under the spotlight. That was the moment my life would be forever changed; the day Usher fell in love with me.

If daydreaming was on my junior high school curriculum, I would've gotten an A++. It was my superpower. Somewhere along the way, though, my powers took a darker turn. Instead of being rescued by dreamy hunks from the horrors of teenage life, I started thinking about death. I went from daydreaming to daynightmaring.

I've thought about death, in particular *my* death, more than I care to admit. If a habit tracker app existed for this, it would probably tell me my longest daily streak lasted one year. It's not a badge I'm proud to display, but it's part of my story. I *am* proud of the fact that I've continued to get up and out of bed, live my life, and do my damn best to make my time in this body meaningful. I haven't backed down.

This story I'm about to tell you is one I've told so many times that it came to define me. I reached a point where I was no longer okay with that and didn't want to tell it anymore. Perhaps this will be the last time, and so I'm going to do it differently. I'm going to tell you how it ends, or rather, how it continues, because I'm still here and my story keeps going. In the early parts of the story, I had no sense that I could get out of the daynightmaring cycle to where I am now. I've learned that we often feel fear or anxiety when we're in an uncomfortable situation because we think it will last forever. We aren't thinking ahead to the time when we'll get out of it. But I am getting out of it.

This story begins on a bridge. It's a weekday in June of 2017. I took the morning off of work to drive 45 minutes across several counties to go to the DMV. I had all the paperwork, required signatures, and photocopies to transfer the title of my dad's car into my name. I am doing this because two months earlier my dad died.

There is a large body of water that separates my county from the one directly south. The Sunshine Skyway Bridge that connects them is a structural icon in the Tampa Bay area and provides beautiful views of the water as you cross it.

That morning as I approached the bridge, I felt vaguely uncomfortable. There was no reason to feel that way so I continued on my way to the DMV. Once there, everything went smoothly as I had expected since I had done my research and was well prepared. I returned to the car to head to work and briefly recalled that moment of discomfort. Should I take the same route back over the bridge or should I go the long way around to avoid it? "No, that's silly," I thought. I started the engine and headed back to the bridge.

Sunshine Skyway Bridge

As I approached the incline of the bridge, that uncomfortable feeling returned, only it was much stronger this time. For no reason that I could understand, my heart began to beat quickly. It felt like a struggle to breathe, even though I was indeed breathing. "Should I pull over?" I wondered to myself. Inside, I felt this knowing that when I got to the top of the bridge, I'd be fine, and pulling over would only prolong the discomfort. I should just keep going. That's exactly what I did. I focused on the music on the radio as best I could to distract myself from the uncomfortable sensations. I made it to the top, and just as I suspected, my body calmed down. *What the heck* was *that?* It shook me up, but I continued on to work, entered the office, and carried on with my day.

Over the next several months, that experience would occasionally return but in a milder form. Not having any idea as to what the cause could be, I concluded that maybe I had developed a brain tumor. It wasn't until I started seeing a therapist that I learned its real name: a panic attack. I developed a fear of that bridge which eventually extended to other bridges in the area. Living on a peninsula on the gulf coast of Florida, there's a lot of water, and sadly for me, a lot of bridges. To date, I've had panic attacks while crossing all three of the major ones.

Years have passed since that inaugural day, and the experience of panic attacks and anxiety has come and gone. I've enjoyed long stretches of time without it rearing its ugly head and I'd thank the heavens to finally be done with it. Then something upsetting would happen, and it would come back.

What was the meaning behind the bridge? I wondered every so often but could never figure it out. Would I ever? What was it about that day in June? I had traveled over that bridge every day for four days while my dad was in the hospital. He was getting better and back to his normal self. Each night I drove home feeling hopeful. The last day in the hospital, my sister sat in the room with us, waiting for the final discharge notice to come in so she could take him home. I kissed him on his scruffy cheek and headed back over the bridge to my side of the bay. That night, a Friday, I slept well. I awoke the next morning feeling refreshed and comforted knowing that my dad was safely at home with my sister. Then my relaxed morning with a good book was interrupted by the call I had not expected to receive. My sister's shrieking voice told me that our dad had died in his sleep. My boyfriend at the time drove us back over that bridge to say goodbye.

My dad died of leukemia, a blood cancer that depleted his energy. He lived 10 months after his diagnosis, initially responding well to treatment and regaining strength. Then his body developed a resistance and he declined. I saw him grow weak. My jubilant happy-go-lucky dad who always had a big round belly that we called "the fluffy bunny" as kids had shrunk before my eyes. One time, he collapsed in my arms.

During those 10 months my sister and I worked together to take care of him. He couldn't drive, so I often chauffeured him to his almost-daily appointments. We joked that I was his personal limo service, and I thought about ordering a shirt with a made-up name and logo embroidered on it.

I didn't have an outlet for the stress this was causing me. In fact, I didn't even acknowledge it. I had to be there for my dad, and that was all I could think about. In retrospect, therapy would have been a good idea but I doubt I would have found time for it. I didn't know much about healthy processing of emotions so it all got suppressed. Perhaps the panic and anxiety was the suppressed emotion trying to release itself. But did it have to come out over a bridge? How inconvenient!

It wasn't just the bridges though. Having witnessed my dad's decline, I became aware of my own body's fragility. I developed a sensitivity to sensations, both internal and external. Bright lights, loud noises, crowds of people, feeling too hungry or full, any uncomfortable sensation in my body, hearing about someone else's scary health situation; all of these things brought on anxiety. This is when my daydreaming superpower became the fuel of my fear of how I might die.

It started with my morning walk. Suddenly I became aware of a feeling of low energy, a little spacey in the head. Not quite dizzy or lightheaded, but headed in that direction. Was it there before or was this a new thing? I had no idea. Perhaps it was just my readiness for breakfast, but this daynightmaring convinced me that I had a blood sugar problem. Perhaps it really was low blood sugar. Maybe I'd become a diabetic like my dad, even though he ate whatever the heck he wanted and I maintained a fairly low sugar diet. Maybe I'd collapse on the sidewalk and end up in the hospital like him. Maybe this is how I would die. Surely it was more than hunger.

There's a TV series called *1000 Ways to Die*. I've never seen it and never will, not with my imagination. In any case, I had unintentionally begun living my own series that could be called *1000 Ways I Could Die But are Highly Unlikely and Purely a Figment of my Imagination Considering my Extremely Low Health Risk, Brought to you by the makers of grief and anxiety*. How does that sound for evening entertainment?

I rescheduled my morning walks to sometime after breakfast, which only challenged my imagination to find something else for the next "episode." One day after an intense weekend virtual health summit for my coaching practice, I noticed tension in my chest. It was probably a combination of stress and excitement from the event, thinking of all the new tactics I wanted to implement, which was both daunting and exhilarating. However, in a matter of seconds I convinced myself that I had a heart condition. "Maybe this is how I'll die," I thought. After about a week of uninterrupted agonizing focus on this rather mild pain that felt catastrophic only due to said focus, I was still alive, and the tension was gone. What was worse: the actual pain or the thoughts about it?

A year and half later, a very close friend of my sister had died. I drove over a bridge to spend some time with my sister. During the drive, I felt the heaviness in my chest again and the fear of not being able to breathe. The next day when I drove home, I felt it again. It really upset me because I had been improving. I was getting so much better, until this happened. The sensations in my chest continued throughout the week. Working from home, there were few distractions. I couldn't help but fixate on my chest and the thought that this would be the last episode of my series because I was legitimately going to die.

I scheduled an appointment to see my doctor. I was so nervous about admitting to him what I was feeling in my chest. This whole time I'd assumed it was all in my head, but what if something really was wrong? I was scared to find out. The night before my appointment, I woke up in the wee hours to a racing heart. I was on the verge of a panic attack and too caught off guard to stop it in time. I just let it do its thing while focusing on my breath and knowing it was temporary. I questioned if it was even a panic attack because I didn't *feel* panicky. In retrospect, this demonstrated a deeper level of trust and safety in my body. I had gone from being scared that any little uncomfortable sensation would lead to my collapse, to being able to relax through a panic attack. I knew I'd survive this. I knew my body could handle it. I knew I'd be okay.

It was easy to see that silver lining afterwards, but at the time, I couldn't fall back asleep, too nervous about my appointment. My doctor put me at ease and performed an EKG. The results showed that my heart was in great shape. He had no concerns. He ordered an ultrasound to be sure, and that also came back normal. While this gave me some relief, it took a while for me to calm down from the stress. I feared that I'd continue to wake up in the middle of the night with a racing heart. My nightmare came true and that did happen a few more times, but I was able to stop it quickly. I was learning how to work with my body.

In fall of 2021, just over four years since my first panic attack, I attended a gathering of friends. We did a round of introductions since not everyone knew each other. This wasn't a casual gathering. We were talking real shit. I gave the Cliffs Notes version of this story. I admitted that I still struggled to free myself once and for all from the fear of pain and what could happen in my body. Would I ever really know why this had happened to me and why it was taking so long to heal?

Afterwards, a good friend who had known me through this entire experience stayed to lend an ear. "I just want this to be over," I told her. "I want to have a normal life again."

"It's interesting that it's about a bridge," she said. "A bridge represents a crossing, a transformation. Who are you on the other side?"

Who am I without my dad? Who am I after going through this experience?

Perhaps I could just make a decision about who I was becoming, and then it would come true. I would become that person and leave this anxiety and death nonsense behind. But it wasn't that simple. It might uplift me and inspire me for a time, but I still hadn't figured out the root cause. It continued to drive me mad. I felt absolutely silly and ridiculous about my fixation on minor sensations and blowing them up into life-threatening disasters, but that's what my brain would do. At times I felt insane and scared that I'd have to learn to live like that for the rest of my life. It's not living at all to be constantly thinking of how it will come to an end. One of the most comforting things I ever read at the height of my experience with anxiety was from Lucinda Bassett in her book *From Panic to Power*. She described people with anxious thoughts as intelligent and creative. They just had to learn how to use their abilities for good. What happened to my Usher daydreams? Why couldn't I drive over a bridge and see a pod of dolphins jumping in the air as a rainbow and shooting star spread across the backdrop?

I used to worry that sharing the details of my anxious thoughts could be contagious. I don't want to give another person a new reason to feel anxious. After all, we have enough fear-based messaging crammed down our throats from the media. But typically, I find that's not the case. If the receiving person does not relate to my experience, they are not negatively affected, and they're able to just be there to support me. If the other person *has* felt similarly, and they can relate to feeling anxious, usually they'll feel more safe to share their experience with me, and together we find comfort and security in knowing we aren't alone. Sharing openly builds trust and increases support. It heals us.

Another common block that we can experience around sharing our authentic stories is not wanting to be a burden. We think others have enough on their own plate and we don't want to dump our own troubles on top. Sure, a time or two I may have left an encounter with a friend and felt the heaviness of what they were going through, but more so I appreciate the authenticity of our conversation, the validation that I'm not the only one dealing with hard stuff. It also leaves me feeling like a good friend, knowing they trust me and that I'm capable of holding space for them to be who they are. My hope is the more we can all be who we are, the more we can all relax. The more we can stop feeling like we have to please or impress others. In that space in our bodies where that tension once lived, we could then grow self-respect, gratitude, acceptance, and joy.

Early the following year, I decided to share all the messy details of this story with someone who hadn't heard it a million times already. Someone who wouldn't find me a burden because I'd be paying her. I sought a new therapist, one with a lot of experience with women who held trauma in their bodies and experienced fixation on pain like I did. She specialized in a technique called EMDR which she included in most of our sessions over the nine months that I worked with her. I credit the work we did together, along with a regular exercise routine, to rewiring my brain. I could finally see how traumatized I was by my dad's illness and death and how suppressing those emotions took root in my mind and body. I realized that my dad was my greatest source of love, trust, and safety. When he died, my foundation crumbled. I had nothing to fall back on. My world fell apart. Maybe the bridge represents transformation, just like my friend said, and I just didn't have a new foundation to land on yet. That's why I couldn't feel safe crossing over.

Don't ask me how EMDR therapy works. All I can tell you is that one day I felt like I was normal again. Perhaps I'd spent enough time caring for myself and, without realizing it, the new foundation was complete and ready for me to take root and make myself at home. The sensation in my chest didn't disappear; rather I could finally see it for what it really was without anxious thoughts blowing it out of proportion. It was just a tight muscle in an area that my massage therapist said was very common.

A couple of months after my last therapy session, I conquered the bridge. When my mom flew down to Florida to visit me, I drove over one of those bridges all by myself and picked her up. When she left 10 days later, I did it again. "I'm normal," I thought. "I'm free! I'm me!"

There have still been experiences that have challenged me, though. Other sensations or pain would pop up, and I'd fixate on them and wonder obsessively about what's wrong. But I no longer assumed I was dying. I understood that the body is complex, pain happens, and most of the time it's temporary. I went on to take walks any time of day that I wanted, no longer feeling scared about passing out on the sidewalk. In fact my husband and I are now training to walk 100 miles across Spain together. How's that for growth and healing?

My dad used to call me Traveler Princess because my big sister was the Princess and I was the one who traveled a lot. In college I spent a semester abroad in Japan living with a family I'd never met before. Years later, I quit my job, put my stuff in storage, and moved to China for 5 months with a friend. I used to be so adventurous, but anxiety caused me to disconnect from that part of myself. There was so much I couldn't do for many years. Even *thinking* about going to Spain with my husband would've been off the table. Now that I feel like myself again, I can be the Traveler Princess again, only now I'm stronger because my foundation of love and safety is not based on someone else. It's within me. Now I'm ready to rekindle my adventurous spirit and step even more fully into it!

I'm also learning to see the strength and resilience of my body, to use my imaginative powers for good, to focus on daydreaming rather than daynightmaring. Maybe while my husband Carlos and I are backpacking in Spain, when I'm starting to feel hungry or tired and really struggling to keep going, we'll meet a fellow traveler who will hop off his bike to walk with us a bit. He looks slightly familiar but I can't place it. He'll lean in and whisper to us, "Do you like salsa?" We realize it's Marc Anthony! Suddenly, his band appears from around the corner of a country road, and they strike up their instruments. Marc belts out *Que Precio Tiene El Cielo* as Carlos and I dance and a crowd begins to form to cheer us on. As if by magic, I'm wearing a blue sequined dress with a red hibiscus flower in my hair, and we're nailing all the foot patterns and turns like salsa pros. My heart is oozing with love for Carlos and this picture-perfect landscape of the Spanish countryside. As the song finishes, the band fades away and Marc leaves us and continues on with his bike ride. I'm back in my hiking outfit to continue my walk with Carlos, feeling like there isn't anything I can't do. My body is strong. I can dance salsa to Marc Anthony even when I'm exhausted and hungry on a 12-mile walk. Not even the dizzying turn patterns of salsa could fool me into thinking I'd pass out and wake up in a hospital. I am so much stronger than I realize. The more I allow my mind to relax, the more my body will prove to me just how much she's got me.

I might not be able to stop someone I love from dying. I might not be able to control how grief impacts me. I may never forget the fear these bridges once represented for me. But what I know without a doubt is that there will always be enough love within and around us to heal our wounds and build a new foundation. May we never give up on ourselves. May we trust that we can always find the safety to go wherever we wish to go.

* * *

Dear Body,

When these thoughts continue for what feels like too damn long, I believe you have something more to tell me, something that needs to be expressed by you and through you, through us. A wave of grief and longing that is ready to be released. Seeing my dad grow weak has affected me more than I ever realized. And I can't be mad about it. It's part of being human to witness both life and death. As your partner, I vow to do my best to listen. When anxiety begins to rear its head, I will know there is a truth that is ready for me to face. Or maybe not even face, but just allow. Instead of suppressing it, I can just allow it to rise up. Sometimes I try to force it. I just want the discomfort to end and so I will force myself to move my body, dancing and singing, to see if that moves the energy up and out. It doesn't always work. The intention is so important. The intention must be to allow, because only then will the feeling feel accepted and safe enough to show itself.

Sometimes you carry messages and I don't know how to interpret them. But I believe your messages about body and health anxieties now are that you want to feel good as often as you can. While the choices I make sometimes may not exactly be leading to a brain tumor or heart condition, it is a reminder that I do have choices every day and it can impact how I feel rather quickly. I believe, dear body, that in the most loving way you know how, you are setting me up to make choices that feel good so for the rest of my life, my entire being will feel good. Thank you body for holding up your end of the bargain.

Letter Prompt

Think of a time your body proved to you how strong and resilient it is. Explore the story below: the challenges and the triumphs. How did that experience affect you?

Above

Remember to look up.

The blue sky stretches on forever. She will always be there looking down upon you. A reminder that we are safe.

Clouds drift off. A blessing that never overstays its welcome. A reminder of life's impermanence.

6

Freedom Dancers

I once crashed a private party for Italian ice, but I'll let you decide if I'm guilty of trespassing or not. The Italian ice truck publicized the location of the event on their website, an invitation for all to attend. By the time I arrived, fashionably late, the guest list at the front lay abandoned, willing me to ignore the "Private Event" sign posted on the wall. I didn't feel guilty at all. In fact, by the end of the night, I knew I was destined to be there.

I walked through the open gate to see a crowded bar to my right. Ahead, rows of chairs sat facing a stage with a raised "dance floor" in front. I watched as the arrhythmic bodies stomped their feet and shook their arms awkwardly. You could hardly call it dancing. Maybe they were auditioning for a Thriller flash mob.

The adults appeared relaxed and comfortable. Only two weeks prior, the CDC declared that fully vaccinated people did not need to wear a mask. I couldn't spot anyone holding a mask let alone wearing one. Everyone sat close together, talking in small groups or pairs. Neighborly. Friendly. It could have been a backyard cookout for a moderately wealthy family, cashing in their saved pennies for a catered dinner and live entertainment. With my mask over my nose and mouth, I immediately felt like an outsider, but I had my motives.

In the back I spotted two food trucks. A-ha! There was the Italian ice for which I took the risk of trespassing! I stumbled through the crowded and cramped rows of chairs, annoyed at the little space the adults left for passage. Arriving at my destination with a sense of triumph, I eyed the menu. They offered a short list of ten flavors.

I'd hoped, albeit unrealistically, that I'd be able to enjoy a gelati that night. I'd had it only a few times at a place that had long since closed down. Gelati is a heavenly treat composed of layers of Italian ice and frozen custard. The custard - so smooth, thick, and creamy - perfectly balances with the ice - watery, cool, and slightly sour. But they had no custard here. Only ice. Was it worth the risk?

"These flavors have dairy, so they're creamier, more like ice cream," the woman behind the little window explained. She and her truck-mate wore branded shirts with the slogan "Be a kid again!"

"I'll have a small cup with two flavors please. Chocolate Oreo and coconut."

"Good choice!" She prepared my order while her partner took my credit card. It's not trespassing if I'm paying for it, right?

A minute later she handed me a cup that looked much too small for my hearty appetite. As I scooped the first bite into my mouth, my reaction jumped out. "Holy shit!"

The woman chuckled.

It wasn't gelati, but damn was it delicious. "I just might have to come back for seconds," I thought. Definitely worth the risk.

To accommodate the line of customers, I stood to the side of the truck while devouring my Italian ice. I chewed the small chunks of coconut and Oreos, marveling over the cocoa flavor on my tongue. Once the bulk was gone, my tiny plastic spoon spent an extra three labor-intensive minutes scraping against the paper cup as if it were earning overtime pay. "Screw it," I thought, as I brought the cup to my mouth to lick it clean.

I spotted a few empty chairs where I could sit, but I still felt out of place. It seemed safer to stand. Then the band started back up, and their instruments beckoned me to sit back, relax, and enjoy the show. I chose a seat near the edge, next to the walking area between the stage and food trucks. The band kicked off their set with the Tom Petty classic *American Girl*, and I relaxed into the comfort of knowing all the words and singing along.

At the same time, an explosion of excitement occurred on the stage, but not because of Tom Petty. Not one of the "flash mob" dancers was old enough to know the words or the song. They only cared that music was playing. Noise! Sound! Beats! They didn't seem to recognize the beat or the rhythm. If you define dancing as moving your feet to the beat, they definitely couldn't dance. They crowded the stage and jumped arrhythmically up and down, side to side, bumping into each other, pushing one another around, stealing hats off of heads and out of hands. Any onlooker would assume they were on drugs, and they were. Sugar, to be precise. The evidence was smeared all over their lips in shades of blue and raspberry. They ran in front of me and around the side of my chair. They almost stepped on my feet and ran into my shoulder. One nearly hit me with a Frisbee!

I braced myself, waiting for the crash that would knock me out of my chair and onto the grass. I waited for someone to scream and cry. I watched as knees got bent and pushed around. Whole bodies fell to the ground and others piled on top until someone retrieved the prize - the stolen hat. As the sugar penetrated their bloodstreams, I watched all hell break loose. I waited for someone to get some sense knocked into them, to realize they were out of control, and that they might hurt somebody. I watched, I waited.

No one cried. No one got hurt. At least not to the point that they noticed. No one thought any better of it until one adult got up to break up the commotion.

These kids had no worries. No fears! They didn't think about breaking a bone or spraining an ankle. They didn't care if their thighs or arms were too fat to be jiggling on the dance floor. They didn't question if they'd consumed too much sugar and might be endangering their health. They burned it all off anyway, but not for that reason. They didn't care what they looked like, and they did look quite ridiculous. They didn't know how to dance to a beat, but their bodies knew how to be excited about the music. They heard it and just did what felt right. They moved. They played.

They didn't think about the consequences of their actions, if an injury might ruin the rest of their summer. They weren't contemplating death or how Grandma and Grandpa might pass on any day now. They weren't occupied with thoughts of death because all they knew was how to live. They were living in the present.

As much as I dislike children for their uncleanliness and lack of consideration for personal space, I envied them. I envied their lack of conditioning from the world around them. They didn't care about socially acceptable behavior, following rules, or trying not to upset anybody. Their minds didn't work overtime to protect them from anything that could cause them harm. They didn't know the fragility of life, the impermanence of being human. Their bodies were too strong, durable, and flexible to know of limitations. All they knew was joy.

"What would it be like," I wondered, "if I got up on that stage and bobbed up and down to the music with them? What would it be like if I traded in my 'sit-all-night-while-holding-a-beer' adult card for a 'run-around-and-play-like-a-maniac-because-it-feels-good' card?"

I sat. I watched. I wondered.

After a few more songs, I stood up, stepped briefly on to the stage to make my way around a congregation of adults, eyed the abandoned guest list one last time, and exited the private party.

That night, wondering was enough. One day, I'd do something about it. I would show my adult conditioning who's boss.

After that night, whenever I'd see a child running around carefree, I'd feel in my body a longing to do the same. I do not know why we don't see adults doing this more often. Perhaps we are too bogged down with responsibilities and the drive for progress that it seems silly to do something just for the sake of doing it or just because it feels good.

Then there's the fear of judgment that can keep us acting in socially acceptable ways. Children don't have this fear. It drives me crazy that they don't obey social norms but it's also what I envy the most about them. Instead of trying to fight my fear of judgment, I'm learning to let it be okay. I'm learning to embrace the awkwardness and discomfort that comes with doing what feels good even when it might look crazy to onlookers.

The best way to practice this is to start with myself. I started dancing more when no one was around. At home, I'd turn up the volume on my Feel Good playlist and let the rhythm move me. I channeled my inner ballerina and tribal woman, creating my own form of interpretive dance. My arms would sweep around me, creating shapes without names. My legs would slice through the air as they leapt off the ground. Flying. Twirling. Feeling. Being. I cannot tell you what it looks like from the outside, but on the inside, I feel like a fucking master. I'm ready to call the admissions department at Juilliard and do this professionally.

I am a dancer.

So are the Thriller flash mob children from the party.

There's no wrong way to do what feels good in your own body. The world needs to see more of this authentic self-expression.

Over time I've felt more comfortable dancing my full-body

expressive dance around my partner Carlos. He'd watch me with focused eyes, smiling, seeing me for who I really am.

I am safe to express myself.

In my close circle of friends, I will dance my art when the music moves me, whether or not anyone else joins in. Sometimes at a park, on the beach, or on the street, I find a moment of bravery and dance, jump, or twirl. When I'm out for a walk and a breeze blows by, I'll throw up my arms and spin around. When I'm on the beach and hear the distant sounds of the sunset drum circle, I'll gallop to the beat, interlacing the hip bumps I learned in my belly dancing class years before. I believe that if I have this desire to let my body move freely, others do too. That motivates me even more. May someone else be inspired and moved to step a little more outside their comfort zone too.

Recently, I asked a woman I'd just met to share something she loves about herself. After she told me, she asked if I'd be willing to answer the same question. Without hesitation, I responded with how much I appreciate my growing courage to dance around others.

I can't say that I feel completely free to move however I want *all* the time, but it has gotten easier. I still envy children for their total lack of inhibition, but I cannot compare myself to them. I cannot hold those expectations to myself because I'm not a child anymore. I've endured years of conditioning and responsibilities that have disconnected me from that way of being. That is okay.

What matters is that I recognize the longing. What matters is that I take these small steps to reclaim some of that freedom. Every chance. Every dance. Every hip bump. Every pirouette. Every lick of an ice cream cup. It all matters. They all add up to more moments where my body remembers what it means to be alive.

* * *

Dear Body,

Last night felt amazing. There is magic in you. After therapy, I saw the sunset and felt a longing to be outside in the grass and enjoy it. I felt a desire to flow. I listened to that desire and drove myself to the park. I thought about doing a short workout of lunges as I have been. But no. You wanted flow. I thought about how I'd seen videos on YouTube about yoga and dance fusion. I thought I might find one when I got home. No, I told myself, I don't need a video to instruct me. I have my body. My body will guide me. I will make it up as I go. I know how to move. This is what we've been practicing. So we did, you and I. We flowed. It was yoga and dance but it didn't need a name. It was just beautiful. The sun went down. The sky got dark. It felt so nourishing to spend that time together. Just us. Just us. I love you. Thank you.

Letter Prompt

Is there something your body longs to do? How would it like to express itself? What would make it come alive? In what small ways can you make that happen?

Medicine

The music starts. Immediately my blood absorbs the beat, transmitting joy and lightness throughout my body. My heart relaxes into the moment. My lips curl into that sly smile when you become one with the music. My fingers snap to the beat. My head bobs along. My torso and arms do some funky gyrating movement that is called dancing in some cultures.

I look at him expectantly.

He takes my hand and pauses for a moment to allow his own body to merge with the music.

We begin our synchronized steps. One step back, two steps forward, two steps back, two steps forward. Counting to the beat in my head, I rattle off, "One and two, three and four. One and two, three and four." Until the numbers become a sensation, a knowing, a muscle memory. The music slips into my bones and moves my feet for me.

The feeling is like being whisked away on a magic carpet ride. Flying through the air. Flying across the dance floor. The wind, the music, my partner all work in unison to carry me to greater heights. My feet remain grounded as my spirit lifts higher and higher.

The other dancers are in their own magical universe. We twist and turn around each other, the shared space a love offering being passed around among us. The dark black sky stretches equally over us all.

I am free yet protected by the structure of the dance. With each turn, my arms soar overhead, my fingertips painting figures of gratitude in the air. The emotion of the song expresses itself through me as my spine bends and arches, back and forth.

I abandon perfection and twirl out of alignment. In my intense connection with the music, I lose count and miss a step. The dance always catches me and brings me back.

I am safe here.

7

Confessions of a Skinny Woman

As early as the fifth grade I remember wishing for a smaller waist, tanned skin, and to look like Jenna Hart, the girl all the boys at school found attractive. Even though I was thin, those preteen years were chock-full of insecurities. It turns out that being thin doesn't mean you will love your body. Those insecurities continued in some form up to the present time of my mid-30s.

Have you ever wanted to change something about your body? Maybe you've wished you were shorter or taller, had curly hair or green eyes. You may have looked at photos of yourself and felt not so pleased about what you saw. I'm going out on a limb here, but maybe at one time you even wished your weight was different.

Despite the insecurities, on most days I love the shape of my body: my slim torso, toned arms, strong legs, and petite feet. Aside from a small chest and short stature, I have a body type that society has glorified.

I am thin.

However, contrary to the societal messaging with which many of us grew up, being thin does not inherently make life easier. It doesn't dissolve all problems. It will not magically make us love everything about ourselves because ultimately, it doesn't matter what society thinks. When it comes to our bodies, it only matters what *we* think.

Regardless of our body type, how our bodies change over time, or anyone else's opinion about our bodies, we all have the opportunity to make our way toward acceptance and love. This is not some place at which we arrive, rather an ongoing practice we must commit to.

This practice may look different for everyone. For me, it involves a lot of listening so that I can work in partnership with my body to keep her strong and healthy. Listening builds trust so we can make decisions based on what works for us and tune out the noise of what the rest of the world says. Yet even if we become fantastic listeners and practice this every day, we still might wish some things about our bodies were different. We might still have days where we look in the mirror or see a photo and find ourselves slipping into self-criticism.

Loving and accepting our bodies does not mean that we love and accept all of it all the time. Everything in life is constantly changing and shifting. It's the nature of our world. Part of the commitment to self-love and self-acceptance is to also acknowledge this tendency to change, in our bodies and our thoughts about them. When we recognize a change is occurring, we can determine how we respond.

Having been thin for most of my life, my commitment to acceptance and love has been a struggle. Yes, read that sentence again. It may sound odd or even like an oxymoron. However, you could replace the word "thin" with anything about any body, and it can be true. Yes, being thin can come with its own set of challenges. While today I have much less of a desire to change the physical shape of my body, there are other aspects that have challenged me to the point of wanting them to be different. Yes, it is possible to be thin and still want your body to be different. I can't say that's the case for everyone, but it's my case, and I'm still learning how to work through it.

Can I share with you what it's really like in my experience to be thin, and how I'm practicing being a better partner with my body?

For one, being thin makes any emotional hardship or ecstasy more difficult. Can you remember when you were a teenager with a huge crush on someone at school? The kind of heart-throb lust that Robert Palmer sang about where we can't eat and can't sleep? All we want to do is lay around and daydream about how we'll fall madly in love. The butterflies in our stomach suppress our appetite and we feel disgusted even thinking about eating. Lust sustains us. I'm no teenager anymore but I've had my fair share of adult crushes that affected me in this same way, minus the doodling of hearts in wide-ruled notebooks. When in lust, I lose my appetite and then lose weight as a result. But lust can be caused by much more than a romantic prospect. If I'm over-the-moon excited about a new project or opportunity, such as publishing a book or planning a backpacking trip, my appetite flies out the window then too.

If I'm highly stressed, such as when a relationship ends, someone I love dies, or I'm nervous over a big presentation or speaking competition, I can barely eat. After my dad died, all I could eat for weeks was a slice of toast with one egg for lunch and a small bowl of Publix chicken noodle soup for dinner.

Because I'm already thin, losing weight is not desirable. Aside from grieving my dad's death, these challenging and joyful times tend to pass quickly but still leave me feeling weak and fragile until my body can rebalance herself.

Then the pandemic of 2020 happened and wreaked havoc on my whole system. That was a new level of stress and anxiety. That summer I worked to build a superbody to keep myself safe. It was a matter of survival. I obsessed over cutting out sugar and processed foods, cooking most of my meals with whole food ingredients. I did anything I could to strengthen my immune system and overall health. It turned out this new whole foods-based diet was lower in calories than my previous way of eating. I lost weight without meaning to. After a few months I noticed my shorts were sagging at the waist. My bras had a gaping space between my skin and the cup.

"I just want my clothes to fit!" I grumbled to myself.

Have you ever been frustrated by your clothes not fitting well?

Being thin, in this way, makes it hard to eat healthy. I have to eat more which means I have to cook more and buy more food. It costs more. More work and more money just to stay the same size. Losing or maintaining weight is tough for many people for similar reasons. Buying the right foods, finding time to cook, and the cost. It's a lot to manage!

Some people may not want to hear the woes of being too thin and trying to gain weight, but what if this was a way to unite us? What if this makes us more similar than different? I know I'm not the only one frustrated about how my clothes fit or finding the right amount of food to eat.

That fall, after nearly six months of my immune-boosting food plan, I went to the doctor for an annual checkup. The nurse asked me to step on the scale. Usually I try not to see the number because I'd rather use how I feel as my gauge of a healthy body. But I saw the number. I was back at my college weight. *Before* the freshman 15.

"This can't be right," I thought. "That's too low."

There I was making loving healthy choices for my body to keep her strong and safe, but seeing that number tripped me up. When I looked within, I realized that I *was* feeling fragile. Being thin can make me feel that way.

Recently my partner Carlos and I visited an imaginative art display outside of someone's house. He took a photo of me in a pretty pink dress surrounded by colorful tiles and shapes strung from the ceiling. When I looked at this photo, I appreciated my glowing smile and the genuine happiness it expressed. But I couldn't help but notice how I looked *so* small, like I was wasting away. Like I had the *skinny disease*. My clothes were swimming on me. That dress looked two sizes too big!

I hate the feeling that my clothes are baggy. Many of the photos I dislike were taken during times I actually felt quite strong and comfortable in my body. It's strange to see something reflected that doesn't match how I feel inside. "Who *is* that?" I ask myself. I've learned it's possible to hold two opposing feelings at the same time, no matter how strange it may feel.

If I feel weak and fragile, I know it's a sign that I need to tweak my diet and eat more or different foods. I check in with my body to see what she wants in order to restore strength and balance. Sometimes, though, I truly do feel great, and I have to change my thoughts when looking at these photos. Strong and healthy looks different for everyone.

For me, maintaining a strong body entails not just what I eat but also when I eat. Friends describe me as someone who's always eating but never gains weight. This is quite accurate, and while it might sound like a dream, it's not all it's cracked up to be. I have a metabolism so strong that often I can't go more than three hours between meals. It took me years to conclude that I should just eat more - duh! But because I'm petite, my stomach is also small and can't hold much food at once. I tend to eat a lot of smaller meals throughout the day. If I leave the house, I almost always bring a snack or pack a meal because I don't know when hunger will strike. And when it strikes, it strikes hard. If I don't get a proper meal in time, I become foggy-brained, lethargic, cranky, and anxious.

I could be home all day with 24-7 kitchen access, but if I'm busy or lazy and do not prepare enough food for myself, I'll be ravenous all day. I will not be able to think about anything else except how hungry I am and how I wish there was more food. Carlos says I undergo a transformation. He can see my eyes glaze over. I imagine it as a transformation into a wolf, where I hunt the fridge and pantry for delicious prey but find nothing! I rarely order takeout under these circumstances because it's never been my lifestyle. Instead, I fall back on cans of beans, nuts, muesli, or a Lara Bar if I have one. But the wolf is not satisfied. She drools and howls with disappointment. She vows that tomorrow she must go to the grocery store and cook, or buy better snacks.

Thankfully, I'm becoming a better partner to my body. If I'm feeling hungry but start throwing out my old excuses, such as not wanting to spend money on overpriced takeout or grab-and-go from the grocery store, I stop myself. I say, "What do you really need right now?" If the answer is "food," then I just go and get something convenient.

If being thin is hard when staying home, then you can bet it makes travel challenging too. I'd love to hike through big national parks out west, which would require lots of walking. Exercise + a fast metabolism + the tendency of travel to mess with my appetite and eating schedule + being stranded in nature with no foraging skills = me as a rather cranky hiker. I don't imagine they have food trucks along the way. I might have to invest in camping cooking equipment and learn how to start a fire. If only I had been a Boy Scout.

On most days, I do eat a lot. Carlos jokes that my breakfast is three courses. Even hobbits only have a second breakfast! It's a delicate balance between nourishing myself so I don't become famished in two hours, and not stuffing myself to the point that I feel sick. I'm still trying to figure it out.

Some days this tiny stomach and fast metabolism stuff pisses me off, and I wish my body was not so sensitive. Some people actually *forget* to eat. How does this happen? My body doesn't work that way.

I will at times think, "Why can't that be me once in a while?" so that I could hold out longer between meals. I could enjoy a paddleboard outing on the water, a hike in Utah, or a leisure meetup with a friend without worrying about when I'll get my next meal. Instead, I bring snacks everywhere as emergency supplies.

Carlos almost died once because of my hunger and insufficient snacks! He wasn't in any real danger but he perceived himself to be. In 2020, he took me to his homeland of Puerto Rico for the first time. We had a mutual friend there named Melanie who used to live near us in Florida. We visited her home which was about an hour away from where we were staying. We had breakfast that morning, then stopped on the way to get coffee and a small ham croissant sandwich. I packed my usual snacks: a meat jerky stick and a handful of nuts.

Melanie was recovering from an injury, so I expected a short visit. We could get lunch somewhere afterwards around town. But it turned out she was in great spirits and happy to receive company. I was equally happy to spend quality time with her for the first time since she had moved back home to Puerto Rico a year ago. If I had remembered how much we could talk, perhaps I'd have had the foresight to bring lunch with us. During our three or four hour conversation, I scarfed down the meat stick and the nuts.

It was after 4 PM when we left. The transformation into a ravenous wolf was well underway. "Carlos, we have to get food ASAP!" I demanded, as soon as we exited the door.

"I know, mi amor, I've got a plan. I know of the perfect place to go." We jumped in the car and I began chatting excitedly about how great it was to catch up with Melanie, filling the time in what I assumed would be a short drive until my next meal. To my surprise, we drove and drove until we left Melanie's city behind. Where were we going? Wasn't it the obvious choice to stop somewhere close by? Carlos had his plan, though. And surely he saw that glare in my eyes as a warning. Perhaps he was taking me to try a Puerto Rican delicacy and show off the best of his island. We drove 20 minutes to get there. We pulled into the dirt lot and saw a few people sitting outside at picnic tables. The windows of the food truck were shut. The place was closed. My chattiness came to a screeching halt.

We were now somewhere halfway between Melanie's house and Carlos' parents' home. There was nothing on the way. We'd have to take the highway. Then after that came the zigzagging route up the side of a mountain. There are no restaurants on that route. We passed up the chance to eat in a city with hundreds of options and now had to go the entire way back home.

I did not say a single word on the rest of the drive. Instead I focused on slow breathing to relax my anxious and hungry thoughts. Carlos knew that he screwed up; he stayed silent too. It was safer that way.

We made the trek up the mountain and stopped at the first place at the top, a Mexican restaurant. "My sister used to work here. They're always quick to bring food." Carlos' words were my only consolation. We sat at a table on the outdoor patio which overlooked the thick mountain forest. It was a spectacular view that might as well have been a crappy painting by a 5-year-old when seen through my beyond hungry lenses. I thought about how stupid it was that I could not marvel at this dream view. If only it were a few hours earlier, I'd have been on cloud nine, smiling with gratitude for nature's beauty. Instead I sat in silence, trying not to count the hours since that croissant sandwich. We ordered our food, then waited a while. I took a sip of water and then another. Other diners occupied just a few tables. "Let me go ask them when the food will be out," Carlos offered quietly as he got up from the table.

It was now 5:30 PM. I'd gone more than six hours without a proper meal. Carlos knew it was bad because I hadn't said a word to him since the misfortune of the closed food truck. If I had opened my mouth, it would not have been kind. Inside, I was fuming! Carlos could probably see the hot steam coming out of my head.

This experience was for the best. Now Carlos knows first-hand what happens when I undergo this transformation. He now lives in fear (just the right amount) and can detect by the look in my eyes when the transformation is coming. He acts quickly to find food and will never again drive an extra 20 minutes when we could drive five. It takes careful planning to cater to my eating schedule. We find ways to make it work, but still, it's annoying and I feel like a slave to my hunger.

But alas, these experiences have taught me to have more respect for my body and to be a better listener. We all have something we're dealing with. No body is perfect. Despite these frustrations and the occasional longing for something to be different, I do not hate my body. I admit, though, that I have not always been loving toward her either. This relationship requires me to continually affirm my commitment to listen, to express gratitude, and to recognize when I need to change course and work with rather than against her. My body is beautiful and miraculous and I'm so grateful to have her. Without her, life literally would not be possible.

I often reframe my frustration as gratitude that my body communicates with me. Hunger is one of her ways of telling me what she needs. And don't we all wish the other person in our relationship would just tell us what they wanted so we didn't have to be mind readers? In that sense, I'm pretty lucky! In her times of weakness and hunger, it's hard to remember this. I get angry. "Why are you so needy??" I want to shout. "Why can't you chill for an hour until we can get a good lunch? I just want to enjoy the rest of this excursion. Then we'll be home." As a kid when I was being mean or throwing a tantrum, my mom would tell me, "I still love you, but I don't like you very much right now." That's how I feel about my body when I'm hungry. It makes sense. Who wants to feel weak and needy?

A body is meant to live and dance and connect with others and with the world around them. A body should appreciate the view of the forest at the top of a mountain. We need strength to do that. I want to feel strong every day. I *can* be thin and strong.

Strength is a commitment. It requires one to listen well to what the body needs. I can see now that while weakness does not feel good, it's part of the same compass that will take me back to strength.

Think about yourself and the other people you know who've struggled with their bodies in some way. Can you find any similarities in all of our experiences? No matter where any of us are with our bodies; whether we wish to lose weight, gain weight, build muscle, reduce pain or symptoms; we have a lot in common. We're trying to find the right way to eat; the right foods, the right amounts, the right timing. We're trying to find what balances us. How many of us do not like how we look in photos? How many times have we just wanted our clothes to fit right? How often do we feel limited in what we can do because of our bodies? How many of us feel so frustrated trying to figure it out and get the result we want? Don't we just want to feel capable and healthy? Our starting points and journeys may vary, but they're only a different manifestation of the same need for more acceptance, love, gratitude, and most of all, listening.

No body type is better than the other. We all have this one miraculous body. They're all different, but they do share one commonality: they're here to teach us. The lessons that we need are different, so we all get a teacher who specializes in what we're here to learn. How beautiful is that? At times I feel guilty for acknowledging how being thin feels to me, but to silence or ignore that would be dishonest and disrespectful to myself and my loving teacher. This is a part of my lesson.

It's time for us to stand united in our experiences. They are unique yet fundamentally the same. It's time to end the guilt, the shame, the comparison, the judgment, the separation, the envy, the idealization of being or looking any certain way. It all needs to end. Let's focus our energy instead on working in partnership with our own body to feel our best. I'm still learning how to do this. It's not easy, but I know it's worth it, and I hope you'll join me in this lifelong commitment because you and your body deserve it. We all deserve to feel our very best.

Me and Cousin Itt at the pumpkin patch

* * *

Dear Body,

As I look at this photo of me with a Cousin Itt scarecrow at the pumpkin patch, I can't help but notice how flat my torso looks, how tiny and breakable my dear body looks. But I'm learning to see this differently. If my eyes see through the lenses of what I really feel, then I know I feel scared of being weak. I must let it be okay to have those feelings and love myself through it, and also focus on all the ways I am strong. The truth is this photo is a reminder of my playful spirit, an opportunity seized to find joy in an ordinary moment. In the next photo, I have my hair pulled over my face to mimic Cousin Itt, my eyeglasses securing the hair in place. I see a strong capable body. What's the difference between these two photos? One weak and one strong. Could it be the angle? Could it be that I know it takes a gentle strength for me to be silly in public? Truly both. But I have stretched myself a lot to follow what feels good even at the risk of looking a little ridiculous around others. Dancing on the beach. Singing in the grocery store. I love that about me, and I love that you, Dear Body, allow me to express it. Together let's continue to play, dance, pose, and do all the things that strengthen our spirit. I Love You. I love you unconditionally.

Love,
Me

Letter Prompt

Have you ever wanted to change something about your body? What if this part of you was trying to teach you something? Write a letter to your body to explore what that could be. When you complete your letter, consider writing a second one from your body responding back to you. Try not to think too much about what you write; just let the words come out without expectation.

8

Spectrum of Emotions

"AAAAHHHHH!!!" I screamed in the car, as I turned on to 6th Avenue toward the library. "AAAHHH!!!! Ahahahaha!"

As I released my frustration, the tight scowl on my face gave way to laughter. If anyone could see or hear me, what would they think? I imagined the look on their face, scared or amused, which probably mirrored my own. I recalled the times my silly father would randomly lower the car windows while driving and yell out "HELLPPP!" just to get a rise out of me and my sister. In my case, the windows were up, and I got the screams out of my system before others in the parking lot could witness me.

I'd just left the Spectrum store to return some WiFi equipment. When I entered the store, I counted seven customers standing around waiting. All employees were engaged with customers; there was no one to flag down. The sign-in touchpad in front of me invited me to join the queue. "Seriously?" I thought to myself. "I don't need to talk to anyone. I just need to drop this off." Being the rule follower that I am, I signed in and took my place as a wallflower to the far right of the room.

"This is good," I thought. "I have some quiet time to think about what I'm doing with my life." A friend had posed a question to her Facebook audience that morning: *What is your life mission?* It would have been easy to scroll past it and not give it another thought, but for some reason, that day it felt important. The pressure of that question bore down on me ever since I read it. How do I answer that? I don't know! I can't tell you! But I've been given the gift of waiting in a Spectrum store. I can sit here, think about my values, and come up with a game plan.

I began to brainstorm. What new avenues will I pursue to share my books? I had just signed up to be a vendor at an upcoming market. What can I do now to prepare for that?

A voice inside cried, "No! Not here! This is not the environment to do this! Not the Spectrum store!"

Another responded, "This is total BS that I have to stand here and wait just to drop something off. My time is precious. I'm having a serious moment here with the future trajectory of my life. I need to get out of here and deal with this properly!"

The rule follower chimed in, "If my equipment return isn't handled properly, they could charge me a lot of money." After fifteen minutes of this heated debate in my head, these parts of me reached a consensus. I dropped the bag of equipment next to an empty register and left.

Backing out of the parking lot, my thoughts returned to the question at hand: What *is* my life mission? All I know is I'm just here trying to make the best of it. I have a book to write, and I know that's part of it. But this book is terrifying. It's so BIG! Our relationship with our bodies is so complex and I want to do this project justice. It's overwhelming! I don't know how I'm ever going to get it together! That's when the screaming began.

"AAAAAAAAAAAAAHHHHHHH!!!! AAAAAAAAAAAH-HHH!!!!!"

Ahhh-hhaaaa!! A-Ha!! I've got it! Yes, of course this is terrifying and overwhelming. Yes, of course it's asking a lot of me. This book is requiring me to step up. It's taking me somewhere I've never been before. It's changing my life. It's growing me. And growing comes with growing pains. I'm being stretched out of my comfort zone. I'm expanding. And this is exactly how I know I'm in the right place. *This* is my mission! A-ha!

Just like that, a few good screams released the tension, brought me clarity, and sent me on my merry way. I got out of the car and deposited the unread George Orwell book in the library book drop. As soon as I got home, I wrote myself a note to keep on my writing space:

> Don't go back. GO FORWARD. Yes, this book is asking a lot of you. It's a big responsibility. It's an HONOR! You are the chosen one. Feel the growing pains, and get to writing!!! I accept my mission. THANK YOU!

With a tendency to overthink and strive for perfection, I'm quite experienced at feeling overwhelmed. When I learned about the practice of screaming out frustration to clear energy from the body, it seemed a bit strange, but for me, it works! It allows the intensity of the situation to come down so I can reach a neutral space and consider the message in the frustration.

The morning at the Spectrum store caused a lot of irritation to build up within me. This allowed me to turn to this practice which I knew would help me release that unhelpful energy and move forward. There are more ways to do this than screaming, though. In fact, I have a list I keep posted in an accessible place in my home as a reminder that whenever I am having a difficult time, there are many ways I can soothe myself:

Scream. Moan. Cry. Breathe. Dance. Run. Write. Pray. Jump. Stomp the floor. Sing.

These are all ways of moving stagnant or stuck energy that have worked for me at one time or another. You may have your own methods, or perhaps, like me not too long ago, you never thought for a second about this. Maybe it seems weird, bizarre, hippie dippie, or absolutely nutso. But hey, don't knock it til ya try it.

Children have temper tantrums all the time. Have you noticed how when a child is upset, they scream and cry and stomp their feet? They carry on for a bit, but then they're done and move on with their lives. Why can't we adults do the same thing?

As a teenager, I had a CD that I had made with the most tear-jerking songs. Whenever I felt lonely or hopeless, I'd put on that CD and cry the ugliest of cries. My face became hot, red, and stained with tears. I'd gasp for breath through my sobs and those weird facial contortions you make when it feels like your world is falling apart. Usually after four songs, the crying would slow down. By song six, I became quiet and calm, ready for a nap to sleep the rest of it off and wake up feeling like a new person.

As an adult I do not cry as easily. Unless there's a cheesy scene in a movie where a dad and daughter hug, or a pig is cuddling with a baby chick. Expressing my emotions is not as easy or natural as it used to be.

Many of us have been taught to keep ourselves composed so as not to fall apart. When my dad was diagnosed with cancer and I was thrown overnight into a caretaker role, I had no space to process emotions. I just had to show up and do the work that I needed to do. I suppressed it as a means of survival. Unlearning that pattern has meant being very intentional with managing my feelings. I have to make myself stop what I'm doing, leave the proverbial Spectrum store, and confront what is agitating me.

Other great ideas not included in my initial list above are creating art, laughing, orgasms, yoga, tai qi, Tae-bo, humming, EFT/tapping, rockwall climbing, massaging your feet, hugging yourself, walking your dog, chasing your cat, playing air guitar, cleaning the house, cleaning your elderly neighbor's house, creating your own Adele choreography, or swinging across the monkey bars at the playground. The body has unlimited ways of expressing itself. You may turn to different practices depending on the situation at hand.

One day, I was feeling nervous before delivering a webinar on managing anxiety. My partner came into the room where I was getting ready and said he had a special practice to share with me to bring positive energy into my session. I felt so blessed to have such a thoughtful man by my side. I sat in curiosity waiting for him to reveal this practice with me. He picked up his phone and pulled up a video on YouTube. When the first chord struck, I recognized this 90s hit right away. The *Macarena!* We stood up and danced awkwardly, laughing together, as we tried to remember the right moves in the right order. By the end of the song, I felt so much lighter and relaxed. A smile replaced the fretful expression on my face. Wow, that did wonders! Not only did the music uplift my spirit, but my focus on the choreography completely dismantled the worrying thought pattern about everything that might go wrong in my session. I decided to include the *Macarena* in the agenda of practices I would share in the webinar.

While I've had a lot of success with these energy-moving practices, I have experienced times when they don't work at all. Sometimes the emotion just needs to run its course, and I can't force it. I've learned it's best to enter a practice with the intention to comfort rather than fix myself. The emotions I experience are not bad or wrong, and I don't need to obliterate them. I can, however, support myself as best as I can through them so that self-expression and feeling becomes a safe practice. May we all feel safe in expressing the spectrum of human emotions in healthy ways.

* * *

Dear Body,

I am opening a new door, a new chapter for us to experience it ALL. I thought I was trading in weakness for strength, but the truth is none of that defines me. I am everything. I will feel everything. To choose one is to deny another. That creates preference, control, resistance. I am stepping into ALLOWING. ACCEPTING. It just is. I will have thoughts and do my best to unattach to them. I will place my faith in the knowing that you are resilient. I just moved my body for an hour and it felt good and loving. I feel like a bigger release is needed at some point, especially after therapy yesterday. I know you hold a lot for me, body, and I want to give you opportunities to release what is no longer ours to carry. The need to be perfect, this will take time - a practice, a choice. I am breathing it out, breathing it out, and breathing in my love for you and the neutral world that birthed us.

Letter Prompt

Where do you notice your body holding tension? Have you tried any practices to support yourself during difficult or emotional times? What new practices might you like to try?

Visitor

The bee circles around the patio and chooses her landing point.
The big toe of the foot perched on the coffee table.
She crawls down to explore the cavity between the big toe and second toe.
I shiver in response to the tickles of her tiny scurrying feet.
Fear tells me to move my foot and seek safety inside.
Truth tells me safety is already here.
I keep still and calm, admiring her grace and beauty and my courage,
Smiling through the tickles.
What is life but a series of visitors?
Miss Bee lingers, tracing my foot bones with her toes.
I watch her with curiosity, and thank her for the message.
She flies off, leaving space for the next visitor.

9

Bloodbath

One Sunday morning Carlos and I found ourselves behaving like dogs. We received our first ever invitation to go sailing. It happened to be Mother's Day. With both of our mothers living a 3-hour plane ride away - mine in New Jersey and his in Puerto Rico - we had no plans. The prospect of an afternoon out on the water had the same impact on Carlos as asking a dog if he wants to go for a walk. He waited at the door with his leash in his mouth, drooling and wagging his tail impatiently.

I, on the other hand, was spending the morning sinking into the couch and drinking a soothing ginger chamomile tea. Like a dog at the supper table begging for food scraps, my expression cried, "Please have pity on me! Life is so hard!" But I wasn't hungry; I was in pain. That morning I'd started my period.

If you're a man or non-menstruating individual, upon seeing the word "period" you may have just thought, "I'm going to skip to the next chapter." However, I challenge you to keep reading and see what value this story may hold for you! There are times when we may not understand each other well or be able to relate to certain experiences, but we can always be more sensitive to each other's needs.

Like a lot of women, I grew up with the expectation that when I have my period, I should be able to do anything I might normally do on any other day: go to work, run errands, cook dinner, clean the house, socialize with friends for hours, run a 5k, and anything that results in productivity and progress. Blood loss, cramping, and bloating should not stop me.

Several years ago, I stopped subscribing to that mentality when I decided to stop popping ibuprofen. Without a pill to numb my body's pain, I could not ignore its request to rest. I looked up at Carlos with my big sad puppy eyes, unsure of what to tell him. I was torn about the sailing trip. It certainly sounded a lot better than wasting a beautiful sunny 73-degree day inside. But did it have to be today? What a conflict! Do I listen to my body and risk letting him down and missing out? Or do I get up and trust in my own strength, despite the circumstances?

In a society that values progress and growth above all else, it's easy to think needing rest is a weakness. Nature would disagree, and she was here first. You don't see flowers and fruit growing on the same tree all year round, do you? Nature teaches us through her cycles and seasons that there is a time for productivity and a time for slowing down. Honoring these cycles within ourselves and allowing time for rest is an expression of self-respect. The difference is the tree does this without thinking. As humans, we have a choice. It takes strength, bravery, and courage to act in ways that go against what we've been taught our whole lives. It takes wisdom to tune out those around you and listen to what *you* need. Nature also reminds us that we are strong, resilient, resourceful. Elephants migrate across Africa seasonally in search of food and water and may go long periods without, but they keep going. When do we rest like the fruitless tree? When do we tap into our strength like the migrating elephant?

A woman's monthly cycle, a time often seen as annoying, restrictive, and painful, could be nature's way of offering regular opportunities to fine-tune our listening. It's a chance to choose inner wisdom over conformity to the outer world. With these practice sessions once a month, it's no wonder women are so wise! Nature has been grooming us all along.

These menstruating days bring pain and discomfort to many. As a young teenager, I recall spending afternoons in bed watching *Friends* with a heating pad snug under my low back and groaning softly to soothe myself. However, I'd still have to go to school. As I got older, I'd have to go to work. No free passes to stay home and rest. Progress must be made in the world!

For many years, I'd pop an ibuprofen to relieve the aching pain in my low back that sapped my will to do anything for two days. Several years ago, I decided I didn't want to rely on pills anymore unless absolutely necessary. I wanted to find other ways to care for myself. That's when I discovered that I could not always power through and carry on about a normal day with my period. My body often desired rest, and it felt good to take it.

In my 30s it dawned on me that I was losing a lot of blood, and I was curious to know if it was a safe amount. For a long time, I used tampons and I would chuckle at how the boxes instructed which size to use based on how many grams of blood they could hold. Who the heck knows how many grams of blood they're losing? How would anyone even measure that? Was this some key detail that no one shared with me, like what bra sizes mean? I only learned at age 31 that the number on a bra size refers to the measurement around the torso. Finally, I understood the difference between a 34 and a 38. But I still had no clue about grams until I switched to a menstrual cup. One day I noticed the menstrual cup was marked with lines like a measuring cup used for cooking. No, this is not so women can cook with menstrual blood! But finally, we can measure it.

It amazed me that I could lose that much blood and still function. For a time, I'd lay in bed and fear that I might pass out. It never happened, not even close, but it didn't seem that far fetched. I reminded myself that my body knew how to handle this. Nature made me as strong as the elephant walking miles a day in search of water. After talking with my doctor, she explained that it can be normal for periods to become heavier in our mid to late 30s. She wasn't concerned, so I stopped worrying. However, I became more sensitive to my body during that time and stopped pushing myself to do more than I felt I could handle.

I always thought that women should be granted one paid day of leave per month from work so they could rest during their period. Wouldn't that make sense? If blood was leaking from any other part of the body, it would absolutely be allowed! Well, I'm not going to wait for someone else to give me permission. I'm claiming my monthly "I can do whatever I want" day. I'm going to prioritize taking care of myself, sleep as much as I want, and eat chocolate. I'm going to work only as much as I'm able to, and I don't care what anyone has to say about it! Who's with me?

As with all things, each month can be different. Sometimes I feel beyond exhausted and just want to curl up on the couch with my kitties and a cup of tea and rest. Other times I feel energized enough to go for a long walk or even a bike ride. The day's activities might distract me to the point that I barely feel any pain.

Then there are the days when a sailing invitation falls into your lap, and they don't take rain checks. I decided to tap into my inner elephant.

"Okay," I said to Carlos. "Let's go." As the excited puppy that he was, he quickly got dressed and was waiting at the door two minutes later.

In the car, I turned on the heated seat to soothe my back as we drove the 30 minutes to meet Manuel at the sailing center. As far as I'm concerned, the heated seat is the best car enhancement for women ever invented.

We arrived at the sailing center and marveled over the sparkly water awaiting us. We filled out a waiver, slathered on sunblock, and got fitted for life jackets. Manuel invited us aboard the tiny sailboat he had reserved. So far the preparation was distracting me from the pain. I had no regrets about my choice.

As we approached the sailboat, I grew confused and asked, "Um... where do we sit?" Unlike every boat I'd ever been on, this one did not have a solid bottom to it. The "bottom" was a thick mesh full of gaps where you could see the water splashing around underneath. Our seats were on the side of the boat; the spot where you're most vulnerable to falling into the water. There were no seatbelts.

We spent the next two hours cruising the intercoastal, getting soaking wet and learning how to sail. With minimal instruction, Manuel crawled away from his post and told me, "You're up, Jessica! It's your turn to drive the boat!"

"Ummmm...I can't do this! I don't know what I'm doing!"

"It's okay, you got it, Jessica. It's easy!" Manuel shouted as he instructed me on what to do.

"But there's a boat up ahead! I don't know how to steer away from it!" I cried anxiously. Somehow Manuel calmly talked me through it. What is it about sailors that they never seem concerned about anything? At least it puts their passengers at ease, but that doesn't apply when they turn the passengers into the drivers! Soaking wet from head to toe and shivering in the wind, the last thing I thought about that afternoon was my period. I was too preoccupied holding on for dear life, trying to not fall out of that small boat, and not crash when Manuel put me in the driver's seat.

Carlos and I returned home that evening like two dogs after a day at the beach. Stinky, spent, and content with the day's efforts, we collapsed on the bed and dozed off.

That Mother's Day was by far (and by choice) the most adventurous of all my period days. But I suppose if I tell my boss, I'll never get a paid day off.

* * *

Dear Body,

I am so amazed by what you can do. Every month you give me the ability to bring new life into this world. While I'm not going to use it, and have often wished there was a place to cast my final vote of "no, thank you" and put an end to this cycle of cycles, I can still marvel at the process. This all happens without my having to do anything. Nature is miraculous like that. My body is a natural wonder! While I may not always be able to easily discern whether you need rest or to just get up and out and do something, I promise I will do my best to listen and change course when you show me the signs that you'd prefer something else instead. While this time of the month does not feel good, and sometimes I worry, I know there is nothing to be afraid of. I know that you, my dear body, can handle this. I bow to your strength and wisdom. Thank you for reminding me every single month how capable and miraculous I am.

Love,
Me

Letter Prompt

How do the cycles you see in nature show up in your life and body? Do you find yourself flowing through or resisting the fluctuations? What can you (or others) do to better support yourself through monthly or seasonal cycles?

10

Me Versus The Muffin Man

I spent Labor Day 2021 worrying about a muffin. At that time, I couldn't tell you what kind of muffin it was because I had yet to see it. It could have been chock full of chocolate chips, plump berries, or chopped walnuts. It may have been prepared in a bakery or a home kitchen. In my state of unknowing, I worried more.

There are two things I could tell you with at least 97% certainty.

One - this muffin would contain sugar.

Two - the next morning some type of muffin would be presented to me at breakfast when I met my friend Nina in the park.

The only reason this presented a conundrum is that I was just two days into a five-day goal of consuming no added sugar.

I'm not one for cleanses or diets. I long ago traded restriction and self-denial for listening to what my body wants, or at least I like to believe I did. I'm not sure if I could ever fully detach from the influences of our extreme diet culture and the overwhelming amount of health information presented to us daily. Whether it's a news article, an ad, a fun beach-read book, or even a well-meaning

Facebook post from a friend, there's always something trying to convince me I can change this one thing in my diet to be healthier. The influence for my no-sugar challenge came from a book, an innocent fiction one at that.

I've had my nose in a book since my nose was big enough to fit there. Given my Italian-Greek heritage, that was pretty early on. Somehow throughout the years, I managed to escape being influenced by the characters and themes of the hundreds of books I've read. This time was different.

This book happened to be about a deranged woman running a retreat center in a vintage hotel and spa. There wasn't any foreshadowing that she was deranged until later on, so for the first 100 or so pages, I found her inspiring. The resort supplied gourmet meals such as vegetable curry and steak with roasted asparagus. The one ingredient intentionally left out from all dishes was sugar. The guests would embark on a five-day no added sugar experience.

A thought crossed my mind. *Wouldn't it be fun to join them?*

One of the best parts of reading is that you can get sucked into the storyline and feel like the characters are part of your intimate circle of friends. This was the first time, though, that I considered making such a change in my own life to bring myself into the story. It wasn't practical to check myself into a health retreat or hire a gourmet chef, but I figured I could manage five days without sugar.

These five days could allow me to detach from my after-lunch dark chocolate fix. I love my after-lunch treat for the obvious reason: chocolate is delicious! It also contains essential minerals, which I feel benefit my body. In the previous weeks, though, chocolate had become an emotional crutch. If a work day felt stressful or I couldn't figure out a solution to a problem right away, I'd get frustrated. My knee-jerk reaction was to go to the secret chocolate stash and break off a piece.. or five. Eating for comfort, in my opinion, is fine on occasion. I worried though, that I was doing it almost every day and using chocolate to avoid difficult situations. I wanted to break this habit and instead allow myself to feel the frustration and work through it. Later, once I had better emotion-processing skills, I could choose to consume chocolate for the sole purpose of enjoying it.

There I was just kicking off this no sugar challenge alongside my fictional health retreat buddies when an evil temptress cloaked in a paper wrapper threatened to derail me. Tomorrow, Muffin Day, would be day number three out of five.

I consider myself to be quite the muffin enthusiast. I've been baking the most perfect muffins for years. My favorite recipes use ingredients like ground oats, mashed bananas, pumpkin puree, and frozen blueberries. When I first embarked on this muffin escapade, I always added dark chocolate chips. I've since perfected my recipes to the point that they don't need them, and that's coming from someone who does not turn down chocolate easily! Not needing chocolate is hardly a reason to omit it, but sometimes I do. Chocolate or not, the result is a delicious, satisfying, and moist muffin.

I doubted that these Labor Day mystery muffins would be like mine. Even if they were homemade and even if they didn't have chocolate, most muffins do contain quite a bit of sugar. Whatever the case, I had less than 24 hours to make a decision.

Do I eat it? Do I not eat it? Do I ask her what's in it? If it has sugar? At regular intervals throughout the day, these questions cartwheeled through my mind.

The afternoon before Muffin Day, I did a little prep work. I whipped up a batch of oatmeal with flax seeds, strawberries, and coconut milk. This is what I would bring to the breakfast picnic along with some yogurt.

That evening Carlos and I went to a cute waterfront town called Dunedin. It was a beautiful place for a stroll. The county-wide walking and biking trail cut respectfully through its downtown. Lined with locally-owned restaurants and breweries, you could often hear live music from any direction. Dogs walked or sat happily with their humans. Evening diners would all head in the same direction down the pier to watch the sunset. We followed suit.

The cool wind rejuvenated my spirit against the 90 degree weather that dragged on into September. I sat on a bench, clasped my fingers behind my head, closed my eyes, and relaxed. I would occasionally open my eyes to appreciate the brilliant blue of the waves and sky before me.

A crow came and hopped around the tabletop used by fishermen to clean their catch. A small hose sat attached to the table, and the crow found a small spot from which to suck a drop of water. Then he'd tilt his head back to guzzle it down. The meditation of watching him and the water created space for mental clarity.

This place is so beautiful! Why the hell am I worried about a damn muffin? For goodness sake, it's not like anyone is forcing this upon me!

As I sat there reflecting, I realized that so many rules governed my life. Some of them are great; they keep me on track with what matters to me. They keep me sane and healthy. Some of these helpful rules or habits include:

Walking first thing in the morning
Eating vegetables and fruits every day
Exercising regularly
Brushing my teeth
Meditating or doing focused breathing regularly
Getting up from my desk and stretching throughout the day
Refilling the water pitcher every time it dips below the black line I drew on it.

While all of these habits were created with the best of intentions, there's a risk of feeling bad about myself if I don't meet the numerical goals I've attached to my rules.

When I stood back and looked at it all, I wondered where I had any freedom. It was my freedom of choice that led me to set up a life like this. I love my morning routine. I love having nourishing food and water available. And I'm sure Carlos appreciates my clean teeth as much as I do. I had to be careful, though, and let it be okay if I didn't always follow my rules. Some work days I might not take as many stretch breaks as I need. Sometimes I have an early obligation and don't make time to meditate or take as long of a walk as I want.

Still enjoying the peacefulness of the pier, my thoughts returned to that damn muffin and the no-sugar challenge. *Who cares?!* I shouted in my head. *This is my life and I can do what I want! I'm not actually in a five-day no sugar health retreat! When the situation arises, I'll choose what makes the most sense for me. I don't have to stress about it! I'm tired of this!*

I opened my eyes back to the view of the water and noticed the thirsty crow had flown off. Carlos and I got up and made our way from the pier back to the town center. We passed one of our favorite pizzerias. Carlos had yet to eat dinner and I knew he'd want to stop somewhere. Does pizza fit into a no added sugar plan? Probably not.

I had a choice to make.

I remembered that all these rules were of my own making. I could do what I wanted. I had nothing to prove to myself. If I decided to eat pizza, that wouldn't make me weak. It wouldn't make me a failure. I wouldn't make myself start the five days over. I wouldn't feel bad about myself.

We entered the pizzeria. At first smell, I knew I would eat some. Carlos ordered veggie and meat lover's. I chose the florentine. We carried our paper plates and grabbed a table in the back. Carlos took the first bite. "Extra crispy!" he said with approval. He knows I can't stand soggy crust. I've turned him into a pizza connoisseur.

"Mmmmmm," I closed my eyes and savored that first bite of crispy crust with ricotta and tomato. I love food. I love the flavors. My signature move is eating with my eyes closed, with a look of sheer bliss on my face as I indulge in the sensory experience that eating offers us. I gave myself permission to enjoy it, so that's exactly what I did. No regrets.

The next morning I found myself seated on a picnic blanket across from Nina. Soon I would have to make another decision. Unaware of my internal debate from the last 24 hours, she announced, "I brought muffins and croissants from Blue Moon Bakery!"

"Ooooooh!!!" My eyes lit up. "I haven't been there in so long!" My gaze dropped to the plate before her as she removed the cloth and revealed a giant muffin cut in half and two buttery croissants.

"This is the Maui coconut muffin. I know you like sweet stuff and this is nice and sweet!" she said with a sparkly grin. "Please help yourself!" I laughed and explained to her my little five-day goal to break my impulsive indulgences. "Well, maybe you'll have it or maybe not," she said matter of factly.

Nina spooned some of the yogurt and oatmeal into a bowl while telling me about her recent yogurt machine purchase and how easy it is to use. I finished eating an egg I had cooked at home and brought with me. Then I cut off a piece of a croissant. I did not touch the muffin; not out of will power, not in obedience to the no sugar goal, but out of respect for my body.

Experience has taught me that my body does not like sugar in the morning. I spent too many years working in a corporate setting with Donut Fridays to celebrate the end of the week, Bagel Wednesdays to get through the mid-week hurdle, Donut Tuesdays just because, and Donut Mondays for obvious reasons. They always left me feeling jittery and foggy brained the rest of the day. I was done with sugary breakfasts.

Why then had I just spent an entire weekend wondering what to do? Restriction and denial had only increased my desire and longing. Influenced by the book I was reading, I had signed myself up for a challenge that didn't pertain to me. I didn't need to stop eating sugar. I just needed to focus on feeling my stress instead of numbing it with chocolate. I had applied a no-sugar rule that had no business being there, and it caused me to forget what I know to be true about myself. I once again had outsourced decisions about my body.

Nina interrupted my thoughts. "Would you like to take these home for you and Carlos?" She offered the paper bag with the extra muffins as we began packing up our picnic.

"Oh yes that would be lovely, thank you!" I said as I took the bag from her.

That afternoon after lunch, I thought about eating the muffin. Work hadn't been stressful or frustrating that day. I didn't feel bored or in need of excitement. It simply sounded good and I was curious to try it. But I was still on the fence. I told myself I would not feel bad about my choice. If I did eat it, I would not shame myself for breaking the "rule." I would not bargain with the promise to start over tomorrow or add five more days to this challenge to make up for it.

My thoughts drifted to amazing women I'd worked with in my coaching practice who experienced this type of shame and bargaining process but were able to shift it. The shame almost always came about from an exercise or eating program. They'd start with positive and loving intentions to take care of themselves, like my desire to break my reliance on afternoon chocolate.

In particular, I remember Leila who took on a 30-day challenge to build physical strength. She wanted to feel better in her body and see what she was capable of when she put her focus on it and stopped making excuses. Naturally, there were days where work got in the way, and she missed a day or two of the program's workouts.

One day Leila told me, "I have to start over. That's my plan for the next month."

I paused. "Why do you have to start over?"

"Well, I'm supposed to do this program every day for thirty days. But I missed yesterday and last week I missed two days. I'm already behind."

Oh my goodness, how hard we can be on ourselves! After just missing a few days, it was as if everything she'd done up until that point hadn't mattered at all! If a marathon runner intends to run the entire way, but needs to take a walking break at mile five, do those first five miles no longer count? Do they have to go back and run them all over again?

Leila's body was probably so grateful for the challenge and consistency. Yes, she *was* building consistency even with those days off.

I asked her with curiosity, "What made you miss those days?"

"Work," she said. "It's been busy and I've had to work late so I've been really tired. We're also getting ready to sell the house and we've got a deadline so that's top priority."

"Ahh okay, so you chose to shift your focus from this exercise program to a higher priority. And you chose to listen to your body when it was too tired."

"Yes..." she responded with hesitation.

"Sounds like you're doing your body a favor. Sounds like you did exactly what it wanted and needed."

"Hmm.. yeah, I guess you're right."

As our conversation continued, Leila revealed that she spent her evenings painting walls, which required a lot of upper body strength. Strength was why she began the exercise program in the first place. Maybe painting walls wasn't the type of movement she was "supposed" to be doing in the program. Maybe it wasn't working the right muscle groups for that day or it wasn't as strenuous as she wanted it to be to feel like she earned "credit" for it. But it was movement and strength-building nonetheless.

We're keeping score but ranking our efforts far too low. We only give ourselves credit if we follow the program rules exactly, do it every day, and finish the entire thing. We think that we've only earned the credit if our heart rate reaches a certain level, we walk the 10,000 steps, or fulfill whatever other metric we might be using. This scenario came up with so many women, and it was one I'd lived through countless times myself.

I started this no sugar challenge because I wanted to stop relying on chocolate for emotional comfort. What does that really have to do with eating pizza or a muffin if I'm hungry or it sounds good? In the end, it didn't matter if I made it through one day or all five.

I know that I will continue to impose unnecessary rules on myself. It's okay and I forgive myself. I will keep forgiving myself, because I'm human and I can't make myself immune to external influences. I can only practice getting better at recognizing the influences and returning to my inner truth and wisdom. When I think of it like this, I'm grateful for the Labor Day Muffin Debacle. It actually proved to me that when the muffin and I came face to face, I made the right choice. It opened my eyes to how imposing rules and keeping score extended far beyond food and exercise.

For the past several years I've been studying Spanish. Sometimes it's a top priority and other times it drops lower on the list. One summer, I took a break from my studies while I was on vacation. My one-week break turned into a one-month break. I felt so bad about losing my momentum. But did I forget everything I learned up until that point? Of course not! Sure, I got a little rusty on the newer material. But once I got back into it, it actually felt like I was speaking and understanding more than before my break! My brain seemed to benefit from that time off. I returned to practice, spewing out complicated sentences without even having to think about the grammar.

Has your brain or your body ever bounced back after "breaking" a rule, or shall we say, taking a rest? We are not machines. Our bodies are living breathing beings! Their needs shift from day to day, along with our energy levels. Have you heard the expression "The only person you should compare yourself to is who you were yesterday"? Even that is misleading because some days our bodies need rest. Women may understand these fluctuations especially well with our monthly cycles. We all deserve so much more credit than we give ourselves.

If you're doing your best and feeling down about yourself because you missed a day or a few minutes or just feel tired, you are not cheating yourself. You're not weak. You're not succumbing to excuses. You're not letting yourself down. You're not doing anything wrong. ***You're becoming a better listener.***

You might feel like you're falling behind, but you're actually so much further along than you know.

I thought about Leila. I thought about Spanish. I thought about the fictional resort director in my book who was starting to reveal some odd behaviors. I thought about my body, which was neither hungry nor full nor in need of comfort or emotional support. It's a body that receives so much pleasure and nourishment from food, whether it's broccoli or buttercream, melon or muffins. It's a body that thrives in a life that's not dictated by unnecessary rules.

Did I eat the muffin? You bet I did! I ate the whole damn thing and licked the wrapper too!

* * *

There is nothing that you need, my dear, to fill the empty space.
Just breathe.

Letter Prompt

Are there any expectations you're imposing upon yourself or any goals you're working toward? How do you respond when you don't meet those expectations or make the progress you're hoping for? What might your body be asking for in those times?

11

The Chocolate Cure

We had just stepped off the plane, returning home from a glorious trip to New Jersey to visit my family. Carlos had just met them for the first time, cementing himself even more into my life. My mom, Grandma, all my aunts, uncles, and cousins. He took it like a champ. It helped that no one pulled him aside and asked him his intentions and when we'd marry and start producing offspring. Thankfully I don't have that kind of family because I'm not the marrying and offspring-producing kind of woman. I have the kind of family that enjoys casual conversation, walks around the lake, and bagels.

The evening we returned to our home in Florida, my bones felt refreshed. Not even the July humidity could hold me down! I took that energy and went for a long walk-jog through my neighborhood. As I finished my cool-down, my path crossed with Carlos who had just set out for a walk. We decided to venture together a few blocks over to the dentist's office that had four mango trees on the property. We went on patrol duty once a week during the summer, waiting impatiently for them to ripen so we could sink our teeth into their velvety sweet flesh.

That night we hit the jackpot. We gathered a few mangoes off the ground that had managed to escape the wrath of the squirrels. Then, I noticed a landscaping guy on the roof and thought we better hurry up in case he would not support our mango rescue mission. I was wrong. The man paused from his work of trimming branches and waved us over. "You want some of these purple ones?" he called down to us.

I looked at Carlos with wide excited eyes. "Purple mangoes?!" I hadn't seen those before!

The man disappeared for a minute. We walked closer to the building. He returned and dropped large purple mango after large purple mango until our arms couldn't possibly hold any more. We walked back home, carrying what looked like the eggs of Barney the Dinosaur. Maybe my family would accept that as my offspring. The fruits of our Florida love!

Usually I get the post-vacation blues, but this transition was going quite well, that is until the pain showed up. When did it begin? Was it later that night? Was it earlier when we were in the New Jersey airport waiting for our flight home? It must have snuck in under the radar. But what I know for sure is that the next morning, the right side of my low back was aching. It felt like I'd bumped into something, which happens all the time.

Several times I've been in the kitchen crouched in the fridge, trying to find something in the back. When I emerge from those frigid depths, I manage to hit my head on the outer frame. I've bumped body parts on the edges of kitchen cabinets high and low. I've banged my head and arms on the bathroom vanity. I walk into coffee tables and bed frames. I bump into objects that are easy to see yet hard to avoid.

That morning when I undressed to take a shower, I turned

backwards in front of the mirror to examine what type of gash I was dealing with this time.

There was no mark.

"What the heck?! How is there nothing there?" Was someone playing a trick on me? This didn't make any sense. No swelling, no scratches. Nothing. Sure, bruises can take a few days to show up, long enough that I can't remember where they came from. But an ache like this surely would have left a noticeable mark.

Carlos attempted to calm me down, saying "I'm sure you bumped into something and just don't remember. It happens to me all the time."

I knew my body, though. I'm so much more aware of these things than he is. He could have worms coming out of his ears and not even realize it. I've heard stories of women who didn't know they were pregnant until they went into labor. If Carlos was a woman, that would be him.

As the day went on, I couldn't stop my mental quest for answers. The pain reminded me a bit of menstrual cramps, which for me presents in the low back. It was not constant pain, rather it came in waves. Half the time I could ignore it and go about my day. But when that wave came, it ached deeply, and I just wanted to sink into the couch and into the arms of someone I love, weeping and allowing them to comfort me. Menstrual cramps can make me feel that way too.

But it wasn't menstrual cramps. That part of my cycle had passed. What the hell could it be?

I had an idea. The only one that made sense.

"I think I have a UTI," I told Carlos when he returned home that evening. "It's only on the right side, which is how it was the last time I had one. It doesn't hurt nearly as bad, but it's the only explanation."

We'd gone swimming with some friends in their community pool just before our trip to New Jersey. The other times I had UTIs were after soaking in a hot tub that wasn't well taken care of. Pools had never been a problem, but maybe the chemicals were off.

The pain was not as bad as I remember from the last UTI but everything else lined up. If you've ever had a UTI then you know there are other symptoms that make it pretty obvious, like burning when you pee, but I never had any of those. Only the back pain. If not a UTI, maybe it was some type of kidney infection. I needed to know what was causing the pain so I could take care of it before it got worse. I called my doctor and made an appointment for the following morning.

"Has your routine been any different lately?" my doctor asked me in the patient room. He'd been asking a lot of questions about my physical activity and routines. He had me touch my toes and perform some other movements to demonstrate my mobility and range of motion.

"I just got back from vacation up north, so I was walking up a lot of hills, which as you know do not exist in Florida. We went on a short hike, walked around NYC one day. Just a lot of walking, which I do here but not as much. And I haven't been stretching or doing yoga. I normally do that every day."

I had made a couple of attempts to stretch at my aunt's house, where we had stayed. Each time I sat on the floor for a child's pose or hamstring stretch, her sweet snuffly bulldog confused me for a sleeping bag and would try to lay down on me. I gave up trying to stretch after that.

My doctor turned to me and said, "I don't think you have a UTI. We'll run the lab test to be sure, but it's presenting as low back pain."

"Low back pain?" I turned my nose up, confused and offended.

People like me don't get low back pain. Young, healthy people who are active and stretch multiple times a day (except when on vacation with a snuggly bulldog) and eat their fruits and vegetables don't get low back pain. Low back pain happens when people don't take care of themselves. And it's most definitely for people much much older than me. There is no way I have low back pain.

"I can prescribe you a muscle relaxer to help you sleep," he offered.

"That's okay," I declined. "The ibuprofen has worked."

"Heat or ice can help too. If anything aggravates it, then of course stop doing that until it's better, but I don't have any restrictions for you. Here." He handed me a few pages stapled together, titled *Managing Low Back Pain.*

I felt the irritation of a woman who'd just been called "Ma'am" for the first time in her life.

How did this happen? Can my young flexible body no longer handle a few hills? Can I not survive a mild intensity one-hour walk in the woods that my 60-year-old uncle recommended?

The only comfort was that my UTI hypothesis was wrong, and I wouldn't have to start a course of antibiotics or other prescription medication. The whole ordeal was so unexpected and outrageous that, despite the pain, I began to chuckle on my drive home. Here I was thinking the only explanation for the pain was a serious internal infection, and all I had was a sore muscle.

"Maybe it was the airplane. Those seats are so uncomfortable," my friend Tara responded when I recounted the story to her. Having lived in China for seven years, she'd done her fair share of flying.

"I was actually really comfy on the plane," I told her. "My body is overreacting!"

But was my body overreacting, or was I?

That afternoon Carlos came home with his sister who was visiting from Puerto Rico for a few days. This would be our only day to spend with her. I felt conflicted. Should I stay home and rest?

"Come on!" he encouraged me. "It'll be good for you to do a little walking. We'll go to *House of Chocolate* first!" He knew I'd never resist my favorite chocolate cafe.

In the car, I sat with my torso rotated to the left, so my right side didn't have to feel the pressure against the back of the seat. It felt better to avoid contact. But then I got up and walked into *House of Chocolate* without any problem. In fact, after a hazelnut praline truffle and a few sips of Carlos' chocolate coffee, I felt pretty good! Food medicine at its finest, perhaps?

After our chocolate indulgence, we drove to the other side of town to walk along the bay and show his sister the new pier. We walked leisurely for a half-mile, admiring the view of the water and the boats cruising the bay. We climbed up to the third floor for an even more spectacular view of the city from the tiki-themed rooftop restaurant. This seemed to be another potent medicine. How could one complain in paradise?

We walked at least another mile that afternoon before dropping his sister off and heading home. My back did not feel any more aggravated than before. In fact, the next morning I woke up and the pain was nearly gone! I couldn't believe I had spent days in anger and disbelief, worrying that my home in the Florida flatlands would prevent me from traveling to any region remotely rugged or elevated. Then, almost as suddenly as the pain started, it disappeared. I guess my doctor was right after all.

In retrospect, the most likely cause of the low back pain was the jogging I did the night we returned home from New Jersey, just before winning the mango lottery. It had been months since I'd jogged, and I went quite a distance for someone out of practice. Sure, I alternated with walking, but I hadn't stretched before or after.

My aunt was displeased when I called her later and indirectly blamed the dog for my inability to stretch during my stay. Don't worry, sweet Bubba, I know it's not your fault!

The truth is my body is changing. It always has been and always will be changing. I can no longer do certain things I did five or ten years ago, like take up running out of the blue without stretching. Perhaps my body is telling me she no longer wants to run. Or rather, if I do decide to run, all she asks for in return is sufficient stretching and that I ease into it. How could I be mad at her for that?

Sure, sometimes we receive signals of pain or discomfort, and it could be something serious. Other times, it's not, and the body is responding to something it's not used to. As with many situations in life, the response could be temporary. Yet I had reacted as if it was permanent.

There are people who run their first marathon in their 50s or 60s. I imagine those people would tell me that if I take care of my body, train slowly, and stretch sufficiently, I could do the same. Not only could I continue to jog and run, but I could complete a marathon.

On one hand, I believe them. I do not think getting old means I have to give up what the young enjoy. At least not everything. On the other hand, I know that I have put my joints through a lot. I did tons of jumping exercises over the years to stay in shape.

Running is not important to me. It feels freeing to run and at times I get that urge. But what feels even better is to honor the longevity I'd like to have with my joints by sticking to low-impact exercise like riding my bike, yoga, dancing, and other non-jumping aerobics. I decided to give up running as exercise for a while, but not because I was giving up on my body or my youth. Rather, I wanted to preserve my precious body.

It was an opportunity to embrace that my body was in fact changing and there would come a day when I wouldn't be able to do all the things I used to be able to do. It was a great exercise in learning to be creative, to find new ways to move and care for my body. Perhaps in my 50s or 60s, instead of running a marathon, I'll participate in a salsa dancing competition. Maybe I'll become a long-distance cyclist and bike for miles to receive the bounty of a friend's mango tree.

These new ways of moving and exercising are not less than. My choices don't make me weak. I'm not a failure, and I'm not taking the easy way out. In some ways I think I'm taking the higher way out. It's easier to force my body to be a certain way in order to cling to what I've always known. It's harder to lean into the unknown. But that's what I'm willing to do.

I'm learning to change with my body. She's teaching me to be more tolerant and accepting of life. When there is little in life that I can control, I can learn to embrace change. I can learn to be a student again. And when it gets really tough, I can self-medicate with chocolate. In these ways, I actually am returning to my youth.

* * *

Dear Body,

It feels good to sit within you right now. I'm glad to be on your team.

It is hard sometimes for me to distinguish between what's best for us and what's best for others. There is so much information and so many opinions out there, so much being forced into my brain that it's easy to be swayed into thinking "This should get rid of my pain." What I'm slowly learning is to be more kind and gentle with you. You're not perfect and that's okay. Some days there will be aches, some days none. You are different each day, just like my moods, thoughts, and whims. But what will not change is that we are together in this lifetime. I do not want to resent you or grow mad when you do not feel well. There are many things I am feeling in my joints from choices I made when I was younger - lots of jumping and deadlifts and poor posture because it didn't matter at the time. Thank goodness I never went into gymnastics! This is my promise to you that I am giving a true effort to being kinder to you. But just like you, I'm not perfect and each day is different. Right now kindness feels easy because it feels good. But some days it may frustrate me and I'll forget for a moment. But please know I will not stop trying.

Love,
Me

Flowers don't bloom year round. If nature can be different each day, so can we.

Letter Prompt

How has your body changed in recent times? What is your reaction to these changes? What would it look like to incorporate more kindness and compassion?

12

The Gift of Bravery

He reached for my hand to stabilize me as I stretched my right leg over the seat. I could reach the pedals and the ground without a problem.

Manuel situated himself in the seat in front of me. Wiggling around to make the bike rock back and forth, he turned to check my reaction. A big smile spread across his face. "See? It's perfectly safe! This thing is locked in tight." He pointed to where my half-bike tag-along with one wheel was bolted into the back of his electric bike. "You've got nothing to worry about. We're gonna have a blast!"

I smiled back, a bit unsure, but trusting. I'd never ridden an electric bike before, let alone a tag-along where I wouldn't be in control. However, Manuel's charisma and confidence had a way of putting me at ease. I turned back to face Carlos, who gave me a reassuring nod and beaming smile from his bike. He was ready for an adventure. I lifted one foot from the ground onto the pedal and grabbed the handlebars firmly.

"Carlos, don't go over 10 for now," Manuel cautioned as he placed his sunglasses over his eyes. “Let yourself get used to it, and then you can go up more. Jessica, we’re gonna start off easy, okay? Don’t worry!” With that, we took off.

Our wheels crunched over the leaves on Manuel’s front lawn. We made our way slowly onto the street, going in a straight line. After the two houses ahead, we’d take our first turn.

I felt my body grow rigid and tense as Manuel veered right on to Lafayette Street. My knuckles turned white from my strong grip on the handlebars. My breath hung in my lungs. We made it through the turn and I didn’t fall off! I exhaled and relaxed a bit. But we were only going eight miles per hour. Was that really a celebration?

The bike hummed as we continued down the residential road. There were no cars or people in sight. Yet. Up ahead, the traffic circle awaited us. We’d have to go three-quarters around it and turn left into Paradise Park. My fingers dug into the handlebars again. They were getting quite a workout.

Manuel shouted over his shoulder, “How you doing, Jessica?”

“Great!” I shouted back. “So far so good.” In truth, I was still a little unsure.

We approached the circle and whizzed through it, the area clear of other vehicles. My body leaned to the right with the turn, but I felt secure. I just had to get used to the motion.

“How you doing, Carlos?” Manuel craned his neck around to check on him as we approached the park.

“I’m doing great, man. This is easy!” Nothing scared Carlos. I knew he was ready to go maximum speed, but with respect, he waited for Manuel’s cue.

“Let’s take it slow through here, guys. The park gets crowded on this stretch,” Manuel cautioned.

To our right, a couple of guys were throwing what looked like Frisbees into strange metal canisters full of floppy chains. The contraption sat on a tall pole. “Disc golf! Great way to spend the afternoon." Manuel offered, following my gaze through the eyes behind his head.

Up ahead, a couple walked a fluffy black dog who stopped for a break while a toddler kicked off on her scooter. Manuel veered to the edge of the paved road and waved at the family.

"Hey, that looks like fun!" the woman said as she smiled at me. I smiled back.

We continued at a gentle pace down the path, weaving around the outdoor enthusiasts who were taking advantage of the perfect weather. We'd become the stars of Paradise Park, as countless walkers and joggers stopped to watch us. I suppose it's not often you see an adult on a tag-along. It reminded me of when my dad would push me in the shopping cart through the grocery store when I was well into my 20s.

The path widened ahead. The clusters of trees broke apart and gave way to the open sky. To the right, a small pond glistened in the sun, attracting a family of white ibises. I observed everything around me, like a front row seat in the movie theater of life. Well, more like the second row with Manuel's head in the way. Looking around him, I could relax and enjoy the view. Nature. People out enjoying themselves. What more could you want?

To the left sat a covered picnic shelter where a family celebrated with a barbecue and a birthday cake. The smell of charcoal and hamburgers wafted into my nose, reminding me that I hadn't eaten lunch yet. I'd be hungry and cranky soon. But for once, instead of fixating on it, I let the thought pass through me.

We crossed over the pond on a small wooden bridge. Ahead, the path split into two. "Stay to the right, Carlos," Manuel instructed. "We've got a short hill to go up, and then we can pick up speed."

I leaned forward as the bike effortlessly climbed the hill. "I still got ya, right Jessica?" Manuel joked, putting my heart at ease. He had a way of whisking me back to my youth, to the carefree me. I was suddenly a little girl out for a joyride with her loving father. If the moment had a name, it would be Comfort.

"I'm going to take it up to ten miles per hour now, okay? You'll barely notice!" The wind felt a little cooler on my face as we whizzed past an empty basketball court. The trees along the path grew more dense, and we basked in the colder air of their shade. The breeze shook their branches and carried a few leaves away to spiral downward around us.

Ahead, the black asphalt ended, replaced with the gray cement of the overpass. We rode the incline with a view of the busy Brad Street below. I gripped the handlebars and leaned backward as we cruised back down, closing my eyes for an instant to be one with the wind.

We landed in a grassy field sprinkled with giant oak trees that were decorated with garlands of Spanish moss. We were a band of explorers who had just discovered a secret network of parks in our coastal Florida city. From this day forth, I declared to myself, this is where we will take our people to recharge our batteries. To breathe the fresh air and delight in nature's miracle.

Manuel turned a corner, and we landed on a residential street of immaculate 3-story houses. Each shamrock green lawn sparkled in the sun, the owners sitting on plots of gold. "This is the most expensive city in the county," Manuel explained.

At the end of the street, I spotted a community of German style cottages painted white with criss crossed rust brown accents on each panel. "How charming!" I pointed, and turned back to smile at Carlos. My grip on the handlebars had relaxed. I could ride one-handed!

Manuel came to a stop and pressed the big red button at the crosswalk. He pedaled us across the main road, and we entered another paved walking and biking trail. "We're just a couple of miles from the town. This right here is the harbor." The whole trail before us sidled up against the shrub-lined waterfront.

To our left, the houses across the street grew even more majestic, towering over us. Their corresponding docks on the water sat to our right. I sighed with admiration. I'd decided that I would never want to live in a house like that. I would not want to rob myself of that dreamy feeling of admiration you get as an onlooker. I'm convinced that's more pleasurable than the experience of actually owning such a property and becoming desensitized to it.

We basked in the sun that warmed our skin against the breeze. The wind blew a little cooler now that we were by the water. Its energy invigorated me. Seeing that brilliant blue of the sky and harbor, a smile spread across my face.

Carlos and I with the e-bike and tag-along

"Take my picture!" I yelled back to Carlos. I wanted to remember this day forever. This feeling. This joy. I couldn't remember the last time I had such fun. Carlos managed to balance one hand on the handlebars while snapping a few pictures of me turning back to face him, my hair whipping in the wind. "Wooohoooo!!!" I called out.

I felt light as a feather. I could fall from the sky and drift slowly, carelessly, the wind rocking me back and forth, cradling me until she laid me down to rest. That is the feeling I would carry with me the rest of the day.

We reached town and parked the bikes for a quick snack break. Manuel turned to me, beaming with pride. "You are so brave, Jessica! Only my nephews have been on this thing. My wife wouldn't even do it. You're so brave to just get on and ride this thing the whole way here!"

Me? Brave?

Manuel's words touched me. When was the last time someone told me that? Me, who could at times barely walk up the block without fear of an anxiety attack. Me, who spent the last several years wallowing in grief-induced worries about my physical and mental health, turning down fun ideas because I didn't trust myself or my body to feel safe.

But today I listened to my truth. Today I trusted myself and this beautiful strong capable body to carry me through a most magnificent adventure. Today I said yes. I took a chance, and in doing so, I received exactly what I needed. Like the cowardly lion receiving his badge of courage from the wizard, I received my badge of bravery.

It is easy for uncomfortable experiences to shape our beliefs about ourselves. One event in time can forever imprint upon us. Seeing my dad grow weak from his illness, at one time even collapsing into my arms, I absorbed his limitations and placed them upon my own innocent body. I became afraid, even though nothing was wrong with me. My body was different from his, but it took a long time to see that.

There is a time and place for cocooning; for patience, acceptance, and healing. Then there comes a time to allow ourselves to see beyond the illusions, limitations, and lies. Whether they were self-imposed or handed to us from the outside, our bodies may have accepted them as truths. They snuck in, unfiltered, and took root within us, playing the role of key decision maker in all we do. Then we may one day awaken to see that they don't belong with us anymore. That's when we can look beyond and decide what's true for us now.

That day on the tag-along bike was my moment of seeing beyond. Up until then, I had a veil of fear I kept so tightly wrapped around myself, but that bike ride tore a hole in it. I could see a new future. From that day on, it was time to see my body for her full capability. I resolved to tear even bigger holes in that veil, to stare right through them and focus on my body's strengths. She deserved to be celebrated. I deserved to be free.

* * *

Dear Body,

You give me warmth, the gift of breath
Sacred touch, delightful smells and taste
I can feel the energy of the earth
And those around me
With all your sensations
I can truly live. I can truly be here.
Thank you, body. Thank you for trusting me with this enormous privilege. Now it's time for me to uphold my end of the bargain.

~me

Letter Prompt

When does your body feel brave and strong? What other qualities are within you that are longing to be affirmed?

whole
brave

In Closing

Dear reader, we've reached the end of this book, but our journeys with our bodies continue. Take a moment to reflect on this experience and what you want to remember going forward. I invite you to use the next blank page to make art with an intention or affirmation for your body. May this cement your commitment. Thank you for being here.

About the Author

Jessica Juliano is the author of several books about self-trust and connecting with our inner wisdom; in other words, unraveling our cultural conditioning to discover what is true and important for each of us. She is recognized for her style of authentic and vulnerable storytelling, as she believes sharing honestly can help us heal and grow. To help others tell their own stories, she offers writing and self-publishing workshops and coaching.

In her St Petersburg, Florida community, Jessica is often seen carrying tupperware, in an ongoing effort to reduce consumption of plastic and single-use containers. She enjoys exploring the great outdoors, expanding her creativity, and having meaningful conversations with her community members about how to leave the world better than we found it. Learn more about Jessica, her work, and upcoming events at **jessicajuliano.org**.

www.ingramcontent.com/pod-product-compliance
Ingram Content Group UK Ltd.
Pitfield, Milton Keynes, MK11 3LW, UK
UKHW041834190726
13854UKWH00002B/524